Crystal
User's
HANDBOOK

Crystal User's

User's

HANDBOOK

Judy Hall

 A GODSFIELD BOOK

First published in Great Britain in 2002
by Godsfield Press Ltd
Laurel House, Station Approach, Alresford
Hampshire SO24 9JH, U.K.

6 8 10 9 7 5

Designed for Godsfield Press by
The Bridgewater Book Company

Photography by Walter Gardiner

Printed and bound in China

ISBN 1-84181-159-9
EAN 9781841 811598

The information given in this book is not intended to act as a substitute
for medical treatment, nor can it be used for diagnosis. Crystals are powerful and are
open to misunderstanding or abuse. If you are in any doubt about their use, a qualified
practitioner should be consulted, especially in the crystal healing field.

CONTENTS

MAKING CRYSTALS WORK FOR YOU

Crystals are decorative, potent, and fascinating. They have magical powers and properties that attract, heal, protect, enhance, divine the future, and much more. By harnessing the unique beauty of crystals, you can change your life; they can bring you everything your heart desires—if you know how to access their power.

Crystals have been used for thousands of years for adornment and to influence the course of life. Ancient peoples believed they were gifts from the gods and their magical properties have been recognized in almost every culture. Some stones have been used since time immemorial while new stones have recently emerged to aid humanity. There is an abundance of crystal lore—if you know where to look for it.

Crystals come in all shapes and sizes. Some are shining and glamorous, and are sometimes expensive, while others are rough and seemingly dull—until you discover their secrets. A diamond or ruby is sometimes overlooked in its raw state. Many stones are tumbled, cut, or faceted in order to enhance their appearance, but they work just as well in their natural forms too. A crystal does not have to be expensive or rare to be effective; size and appearance matter little when it comes to crystal power. Quartz, which is found all over the world, is the most common crystal. It has considerable powers. Quartz, and other crystals, are available as single or cluster pieces, or are formed into wands, balls, candleholders, and the like. This book reveals how to use them in order to obtain their maximum effect.

NEAR RIGHT Polished and unpolished Rhyolite.

FAR RIGHT A huge, naturally shaped Cathedral Quartz.

6

CRYSTAL ENERGIES

Crystals have many uses; they generate, store, regulate, transmit, and absorb energy. They attract and repel. Putting out "good vibes," they harmonize the atmosphere of your body; taking in energy, they cleanse the environment and your aura.

ENERGY TRANSMITTERS

Crystals have an orderly, lattice-like internal crystalline structure. The exact structure is unique to each type, which is how crystals are identified. Many black crystals, such as Black Tourmaline, have a structure that absorbs energy. This means that the crystal holds on to detrimental energies such as electromagnetic "smog," or negative thoughts, which is good news because this means that the crystal can counteract these negative forces.

ABOVE Quartz can be used to transmit and to amplify energy. Natural Quartz is more potent than industrially produced Quartz.

Quartz transmits and amplifies energy, which is why industry has many uses for it. Nowadays, industry makes most of the crystals it needs. Purpose-made crystals are state-of-the-art; they go into space and are used in the cutting edge of technology and medicine. However, Quartz is even more potent in its natural form.

HOW CRYSTALS FORM

Some crystals are manufactured in a laboratory, but most have been produced over eons by immense pressures deep within the Earth. They are formed out of mineral solutions or gases from the molten core. Some have been heated and cooled, and reheated again; others result from the gradual breakdown of rocks. How the crystal formed affects its appearance and internal structure. Obsidian, for example, looks like glass. It is solidified lava that cooled so fast that there was no time for separate crystallization. A slower cooling process produces crystals such as Topaz, Kunzite, or Garnet, in "pockets," within previously molten rock.

LEFT The natural forces that produce crystals are constantly at work. Most crystals have been formed out of the mineral solutions or gases built up over eons in the Earth's molten core. The type of crystal depends on the way in which it was formed.

Fluorite crystals on a matrix of other rocks. The crystals formed in air pockets as the molten rock cooled. Different minerals separated out as different types of crystal.

CHOOSING YOUR CRYSTAL

Ideally, your crystal will choose you! You may be gifted with one from a friend. You may pass a crystal store and be drawn in, "called" by a crystal. Stand in a store and look around: the crystal that your eye alights on is the one for you. Or, you can put your hand into a tub of crystals: one will stick to your hand. You may find a crystal while out walking. You could also note which crystals attract you most as you glance through this book.

The Crystal Directory will help you to find exactly the right stone for your purpose, and tell you where to place it for maximum effect. Some crystals need to be worn close to the skin for long periods; others need to be placed on energy centers known as the chakras for a much shorter time or held in your hands. Throughout the book there are instructions for specific placements to aid you.

HOW CRYSTALS WORK FOR YOU

Crystals have a subtle but measurable electromagnetic field, and so does your body. This means energy can be transferred between the two. You absorb beneficial energies from the crystal, and it draws off baneful energies from you. Simply holding a Quartz crystal instantly doubles the size of your biomagnetic field (your aura). It can also repair and replenish your aura if it is weak, as do many other crystals. This means that crystals make excellent healing tools, not only for you but for your pets and your enviroment. They are protective too; wearing one keeps you safe.

Crystals can be programed to radiate good vibes out into your environment, which makes them ideal for enhancing your home, car, or workplace. They can also attract prosperity, love, and friendship into your life.

RIGHT There are many different ways in which crystals can be used. Some crystals need only be held in your hands for a short time in order to begin transferring positive energies and drawing away negative ones.

9

CRYSTAL SHAPES

ABOVE A large Quartz Point, machine-cut and polished to shape.

Crystals come in all shapes and sizes. Some occur naturally, while others have been specially shaped to enhance their beauty or their properties. Crystals direct energy in different ways according to their exterior geometry. It is important to select the right shape of crystal for the work you want it to do. A crystal cluster, for example, has a different effect from a single point, or from a geode, even when it is the same type of stone.

GEODE
Cavelike interior contains the energy within it.

CLUSTER
Radiates energy out from the points to the surrounding environment. Useful for cleansing or enhancing the energies in a room.

SINGLE POINT
Focuses energy. Can be used to work on a specific point, either putting energy in or drawing energy out as appropriate.

LAZER WAND/LONG POINT
Focuses energy in a straight line, particularly useful for healing or ritual work. Most wands are artificially shaped, but naturally formed, longpointed crystals such as the powerful Laser Quartz can be used.

"VOGEL-TYPE" WAND
Specially created "indented facets" down the sides of a Quartz wand. Shorter, fatter end is female and draws energy in; longer, thinner end is male and transmits energy out in a strongly focused beam.

DOUBLE TERMINATED
Balances and integrates spirit and matter. Aids telepathy. Treats addictions.

EGG
Pointed end for pressure-type therapies. Detects and heals blockages in the body.

BALL
Emits energy in all directions equally. Can be used as a window to the past or future.

PYRAMID
Focuses energy tightly through the apex.

TANTRIC TWIN (see page 62)
Two crystals growing from the same base. Attracts love. Holds the secret of true union.

SQUARE
Consolidates energy.

ELESTIAL
Small crystals over a multilayered crystal. Flowing energy, gently removes blockages and fear, balancing polarities.

PHANTOM
Ghostlike crystal within a larger crystal. Points the way to growth and evolution.

GEODE

CLUSTER

LONG POINT

DOUBLE TERMINATED

LAZER WAND

"VOGEL-TYPE" WAND

SQUARE

EGG

PHANTOM

BALL

ELESTIAL

PYRAMID

CRYSTAL MAGIC

Do you want to put a spark into your love life, attract abundance, or get that new job? You can! Let the magic of crystals work for you. Ancient peoples believed that crystals had a spirit that acted as a mediator between worlds, bringing things into being. This is what magic is: manifestation in action. Shamans and magicians have used crystals for thousands of years. Spells and incantations are affirmations of intent. While intent can be dressed up with hocus pocus, it works best when spoken plainly with focused concentration. Which is where crystals come in.

The sheer beauty of a crystal mesmerizes the mind and puts the beholder in the right mental space for magical work. The marvelous shapes and colors that are the outer form of the crystal are mirrored by an inner lattice that picks up, amplifies, and transforms energy. This is why crystals are excellent tools for magic of all kinds. They hold the vibrations of thoughts and intentions—and put them to work for you. Purpose-made magical tools such as crystal wands or balls will focus energy and transmit it to manifest in the future, but any crystal has the same power.

When working magic, always remember that it should never be used with ill intent—the energies rebound onto the sender. Use your crystals with love and they will repay you with all you desire.

RIGHT Specially-shaped Obsidian
(above) and Rose Quartz (below) wands.

FAR RIGHT Aqua Aura.

WORKING A CRYSTAL RITUAL

Although magic may seem supernatural, it is actually a natural force. The internal lattice structure of crystals makes them particularly appropriate for amplifying energy and creating the future. All crystals have magical properties but some have been used this way for thousands of years. Clear Quartz, which enhances psychic vision, has been used for scrying—looking into the future—almost since humankind began. Beryl is traditionally used for ritual magic and its sister-mineral, the much rarer Cat's Eye, was the magician's choice to top his thaumaturgical staff. If you fear that you have come under a magician's influence, Emerald renders this ineffective.

CRYSTAL BALLS

You can choose any crystal you like for working your magic. You may select a crystal wand that focuses the energy to a beam (and should be pointed with great care) or a ball that creates a window into another time.

Small pieces of crystal work just as well, however. Crystals can be left in their natural, often rough, state or tumbled for a smooth effect. Pick one that resonates with your hopes and wishes (see the Crystal Directory).

WORKING A CRYSTAL RITUAL

Rituals are sacred as well as powerful. They need to be respectfully approached for them to work well and repeated regularly to be at their most potent. You can devise a ritual for almost any purpose, using appropriate crystals. The ritual described here is to bring more love into your life and uses Rose Quartz and Amethyst. (Amethyst is used to quieten the power of Rose Quartz, otherwise you may find you have several suitors knocking on your door!)

The crystals you use should be dedicated and pre-programed beforehand (see page 16). It is traditional to wear clean clothes when working a ritual. Burning a smudge or joss stick prepares the room. Candles set the scene. Appropriate background music aids your concentration. Consciously make your movements slow and deliberate, moving with intent.

RIGHT A ritual invoking love. When performing a crystal ritual, it is important that you take care to prepare the scene properly beforehand. Your choice of clothing, background music, and candles all contribute to creating an appropriate atmosphere. These details are as much a part of the process as the ritual itself.

CRYSTAL WANDS

Invoking Love

For this ritual you need four pieces of Rose Quartz and a large Amethyst.
You also need candles and candleholders—which could be fashioned
from Rose Quartz.

1 *Place your crystals and four candles on a table covered with a silk cloth. Place one candle to the north, welcoming the spirits of that direction as you light it. Then place the others to the south, east, and west, again welcoming the spirits of each direction as you light each candle. Ask that these spirits act as guardians and keep you safe.*

2 *Take your Rose Quartz crystals into your hands and sit facing your table (if the crystals are large, do one at a time). Close your eyes and quietly attune to the crystals. Let their energy flow through your hands, up your arms, and into your heart. As the energy reaches your heart, feel it open and expand.*

Touch the crystals to your heart. Rose Quartz is a powerful heart cleanser and healer so allow your heart to be purified by the energies of the crystals.

3 *Then say, out loud: "I am a magnet for love. I welcome love into my heart." Place the crystals around the Amethyst on the table and say out loud: "And love into my life." Sit quietly for a few moments with your eyes focused on the crystals. When you are ready to complete the ritual, get up and blow out each candle in turn saying: "I send your light and love into the world." Either leave the crystals on the table or place them around your bed.*

15

MAGNETIZING YOUR CRYSTAL

For a crystal to work its magic, it must be magnetized to your energies. This aligns the crystal to your intent. It helps focus upon precisely what you want your crystal to do and ensures that the crystal will carry out its task. It is intention that makes magic work. Dedicating a crystal greatly enhances the effectiveness of the crystal and ensures that good comes from its use. Select a crystal that is in harmony with your purpose. The Directory at the end of this book will help you to find exactly the right one. A crystal first needs to be cleansed (see page 77). The next step is to dedicate it.

LEFT Dedicating a crystal. Once you have selected and cleansed the appropriate crystal for your purpose, it must be dedicated in order to insure its effectiveness.

DEDICATION

Holding the crystal in the palm of your hand, picture it surrounded by white light. (Hold it in candle- or sunlight if you find visualizing light difficult.) When light is shimmering all around the crystal, state firmly and clearly that the crystal is dedicated to the highest good and will be used in light and love.

Energy can be depleted if a crystal has been sitting in a store waiting for you. You may like to leave your crystal in sunlight or moonlight to re-energize it before moving on to programing.

PROGRAMING YOUR CRYSTAL

Before you program your crystal, spend a few minutes formulating your intent. What exactly do you want this crystal to do? Do you want love, prosperity, a new dress? Do you want to be successful in a job interview? Do you need healing? Be specific. Asking for love might bring you a dog who adores you rather than the man you were hoping for. The words you use should be precise, exactly specifying your intent. They work best in the present tense. So, if it's love you are after, try something

ABOVE

During programing it is essential to be specific about what you want the crystal to do. When programming for dowsing, state that it will always speak true

LEFT Some people find it more convenient to keep their crystals in a pocket, where it will be close to hand.

You might like to make a time each day when you sit with your crystal. Doing this at the same time every day will build up magical resonance. Sit quietly with your crystal in your hands and let the energies flow into you. For healing, place it on the appropriate part of your body and leave for 15 minutes or so. Close your eyes and picture your intention actually happening—that dream man walking into the room, for example. When you have finished, return the crystal to its place.

AFFIRMATIONS

Affirmations can magically change your life. They are statements of intent phrased "in the now." An example of a positive affirmation is: "I attract love and my ability to do so grows with each day that passes." If you hold a Carnelian, Labradorite, or Selenite as you repeat your affirmation several times a day, you will soon notice a dramatic difference.

along the lines of "This crystal always attracts exactly the right man/woman for me: loving, passionate, committed, mutually supportive, creative, and fun." Special requests should be included. Keep it positive. When programing a pendulum for dowsing or crystals for scrying, be sure to ask that it will always speak true, with clarity.

When you are ready, make sure you will not be disturbed. You might like to burn a candle. Sit quietly and hold the crystal in the palm of your hands. Focus your eyes on the crystal and let yourself attune to its energy. Be in total harmony with the stone. Let yourself be open to any intuitive guidance that may come through to you. When you are ready, firmly and clearly state your intention for this crystal. Repeat your intention several times to anchor it into the stone. When you have finished, put the crystal down and take your attention away.

USING YOUR CRYSTAL

Now that your crystal has been imbued with power, decide if you want to wear it around your neck or in your pocket, or to keep it in a special place—you will find suggestions for auspicious placements throughout this book.

RIGHT There are lots of different ways of keeping your crystal with you. One popular way of wearing a crystal is to hang it as a pendant around your neck.

CRYSTAL REVELATIONS

Crystals help you to find guidance for the future. The form with which most people are familiar is the crystal ball, but small, tumbled stones are equally effective. Clear Quartz is one of the most effective scryers.

AMETHYST

FRAMING QUESTIONS

No matter which method you choose, how you frame questions greatly affects the answers you receive. Woolly, unfocused questions cannot result in pertinent answers. Closed questions that demand a "yes" or "no" answer do not move you forward or offer insights. There may be situations when you need a definite answer like this, but your query will probably need to probe deeper if you are to gain the maximum benefit. If you ask questions that are open to guidance, something new unfolds.

As you frame your question, be conscious that you are seeking insight and clarity. Are there hidden factors that affect the outcome? Be aware that answers come at different levels and that precise timing is difficult. "Soon" could be the next day or within days,

or weeks. If a question is answered at another level, replies such as "Yes" may not pan out in quite the way you expected! "Love awaits" may mean that you are about to find a faithful companion: a dog or cat. How clearly you are able to understand a subtle reply depends on how well your intuition is functioning, and this is an ability that crystals can enhance (see page 24).

Useful Questions

Please give me guidance as to whether I should... [specify]

What lies behind ... [this situation]?

Please clarify... [this situation]

Please give me insight into ... [specify]

Please show me how to resolve this situation ... [specify]

What will be the outcome of ... [specify]?

What would be a good course of action for me?

BELOW These Quartz crystal shapes can be used for scrying, but any crystals can be used.

RED JASPER

UNAKITE

CRYSTAL MEANINGS

Crystals have traditional meanings associated with them. For a quick answer to a question, place a selection of the crystals listed below in a bag. Concentrate on your question. Pick out a crystal at random; look at the meanings associated with that crystal to find your answer. If two or three fall into your hand, read all the meanings.

RIGHT Picking a crystal from a bag. When asking a question of the crystals in this way, remember to be specific.

Traditional Meanings

AMETHYST *A life change and shift in consciousness. Faithfulness in love, freedom from jealousy.*

AGATE *Worldly success or a pleasant surprise. Good health, wealth, and long life. Particularly lucky for people connected with the land.*

BLUE LACE AGATE *Healing is needed.*

BLACK AGATE *Courage and prosperity.*

RED AGATE *Health and longevity are yours.*

BLOODSTONE *Unpleasant surprise, unlikely to be an illness.*

RED JASPER *Pay attention to earthly affairs.*

AVENTURINE *Future growth and expansion are possible.*

GARNET *A letter is on its way.*

CITRINE *Celestial wisdom is advising you.*

DIAMOND OR CLEAR QUARTZ *Permanence. Business advancement. If the crystal loses its sparkle, betrayal.*

EMERALD *Fertility or a secret admirer. If color pales, love is fading.*

HEMATITE *New opportunities await.*

JADE *Immortality and perfection.*

LAPIS LAZULI *Divine favor is yours.*

QUARTZ *Be sure to clarify issues.*

ROSE QUARTZ *Love and self-healing.*

SNOW QUARTZ *Profound changes are coming.*

RUBY *Power and passion, good fortune and friendship, but beware strangers.*

SAPPHIRE *Truth and chastity. The past will catch up with you.*

SNOWFLAKE OBSIDIAN *End of challenging time.*

TIGER'S EYE *All is not as it appears to be.*

UNAKITE *Compromise and integration*

OPAL *Death or endings. If the crystal loses its brilliance, an unfaithful lover.*

SARDONYX *A wedding may be in the offing.*

TOPAZ *Exercise caution.*

TURQUOISE *A journey is imminent.*

SNOWFLAKE OBSIDIAN

BLUE LACE AGATE

SCRYING

Scrying is the ancient art of using crystals for guidance. A crystal provides a gateway into the future—or the past. It has the effect of focusing the mind, letting it move beyond ordinary consciousness.

SELECTING A CRYSTAL BALL

According to tradition, crystals balls should be gifted to you but you may prefer to choose your own. Crystal shops usually have a good selection. Weigh several in your hands. Look into them with slightly unfocused eyes. The flaws and planes within the crystal may well trigger images. Note what you can see. The ball that lingers in your hands longest will be the one for you.

ABOVE When not in use, it is best to keep your crystal ball in a cloth to protect it from damage.

PERFECT SCRYING BALLS
Clear Quartz, Smoky Quartz, Amethyst, Beryl, Obsidian, Selenite

MAGNETIZING YOUR BALL
First cleanse your ball (see page 77), then magnetize it to your vibrations (see page 16). Program it always to speak true—and with clarity. Wrap your ball in a cloth when not in use. Unless you are reading for them, do not let other people touch the ball because it will pick up their vibrations. If someone does handle it, cleanse and remagnetize it to your energies before using it again.

LEFT When using your crystal ball, do not try to force images into your mind. Gaze at the ball, noticing whatever images, thoughts, or emotions may pass through your mind.

USING YOUR CRYSTAL BALL

A crystal ball can work on a subtle level, stimulating your intuition. Do not try to find images. Simply gaze at the ball and notice what thoughts pass through your mind, what insights about your life rise up, what feelings you have. Allow these thoughts and sensations to guide you.

Any crystal can help you to scry. Letting your eyes explore a large cluster of Quartz, Apophyllite, or Amethyst can bring powerful insights. Holding it to the third eye or placing one of the crystals listed overleaf in your pocket before you scry can activate your abilities and help you to tune in.

Settle down where you will not be disturbed and take the ball into your hands. Hold it for a few moments so that it becomes charged to your energy (if you are reading for someone else, let that person hold it). If you have a specific question, focus on this. Now place the ball on a stand or cloth in front of you.

Let your eyes go out of focus and your intuition come into focus. Look obliquely at the ball. Let your vision wander into its depths. Keep your eyes relaxed. Images may appear within the ball itself, or in your mind's eye. Do not try to understand the meaning, simply observe. Note what you see, even if it appears to be meaningless. You quickly acquire the art of "seeing." If you are reading for someone else, share exactly what you saw for this may have immediate impact. Refer to the table of traditional symbols or to a good book on symbology. You will develop your own meanings as your intuition strengthens.

ABOVE An Apophyllite cluster. This will help enhance your scrying skills.

Traditional Symbols

Image	Positive Interpretation	Negative Interpretation
EYE	Good luck	Bad luck
MOON	New Growth	Disappointment
STAR	Success	Warning
GLOBE	Travel	Standstill
CAT	Good prospects	Trouble
DOG	Trustworthy friends	Deceitful friends
SNAKE	Learning	Betrayal
BIRD	A message	Escapism
HOUSE	Well-being	Financial problems
TREE	Settling down	Loss
WHEEL	Travel	Injury

LAPIS LAZULI

21

THE SCRYING WHEEL

LEFT Pulling a stone at random and dropping it onto the scrying wheel can provide deep insights.

The scrying wheel enables you to find answers to questions in all areas of your life. If you want to know if your dream lover draws near, for instance, the wheel can reveal this. On the other hand, the wheel may also indicate that there is something within you that is holding you back from accepting love. It may encourage you to accept a proposal— or to think things through more carefully.

USING THE WHEEL

You can use a crystal that resonates with your query—Agate for a money question, Rose Quartz for love, Snowflake Obsidian for possible change, and so on. Or, place several crystals in a bag and draw one out. The stone itself may be significant (see page 19). You may like to keep one or two crystals specifically for the scrying wheel since the more attuned to your energies the stones become, the more precise the answer you receive. Ideal crystals would be tumbled pieces of Azurite, Amethyst, Beryl, Quartz, or Lapis Lazuli.

If this is the first time you have used the wheel, program your crystal to "speak true" (see page 17).

Formulate your question carefully (see page 16). Be as specific as possible.

Holding the crystal in your hands, concentrate on your question for a moment or two, and then, with eyes closed, let the crystal drop onto the wheel.

Read the answer beneath the crystal. If it lands on two sections, both answers apply.

If you have a "when" question, use the timing strip rather than the wheel.

The Scrying Wheel and Timing Strip

Follow your heart's desire

Face up to the past

New possibilities are opening up

Go for it!

Let go

Follow your instincts

Be Patient

Yes

No

Take a chance

Love is available if you really want it

Love awaits

Maybe

Unwise

Beware

Hidden forces are at work

Prosperity follows

Hold back

Do the unexpected to succeed

Think carefully about what you really want

| Today | One Week | One Month | One Year | Longer | Never |

DEVELOPING YOUR INTUITION

Intuition is your sixth sense, a knowing that goes beyond the confines of your everyday mind. Developing your intuition not only amplifies your ability to work magic and obtain guidance for the future, it also enhances every aspect of your life. Intuition means that you can access hidden knowledge, recognize the right path or action to take, and instinctively do what is right for you.

CRYSTALS TO ENHANCE INTUITION

Intuition enables you to take great leaps into the unknown and find the answers you seek. If your intuition is honed, your ability not only to read crystals but also to connect to your own inner guidance is amplified. You can heighten your intuition by holding one of the following crystals to your third eye (between your eyebrows) for a few moments daily, especially before you begin scrying or when you are unsure which path to take. *Amethyst, Yellow Calcite, Lapis Lazuli, Moonstone, Star Sapphire, Apophyllite, Amazonite, Selenite, Celestite, Sodalite, Smoky Quartz, Azurite, Lavender Smithsonite, Azeztulite, Petalite, Phantom Quartz, Ametrine, Aqua Aura, Kyanite, Apatite, Antacamite.*

KYANITE ON QUARTZ

ANTACAMITE

ABOVE Some crystals are shaped so that they will rest on the third eye comfortably. Others may need to be held in cupped hands.

AMETRINE

BLUE APATITE

YELLOW APATITE

MEDITATION

Regular meditation enhances the intuition and allows you to get to know your crystals better. Crystals are a wonderful aid to meditation. Their energy, color, and form lend themselves to quietening the mind and entering sacred space. Crystals such as Blue Selenite or Rhomboid Calcite help you to shut off mind-chatter, bringing you to a point of stillness, as does Kyanite. Lapis Lazuli and Turquoise enhance the meditative state. Stones such as Azeztulite, Antacamite, and Petalite take you to another dimension. Azeztulite places you in a protective spiral that integrates your spiritual essence within your physical body;

RIGHT The energy, color, and form of crystals make them particularly well suited to aiding meditation. Placing certain crystals on your third eye can heighten your intuition.

QUARTZ

Dark Smoky Quartz may be naturally or artifically irradiated. The 'black' Smoky Quartz below left is artifically irradiated and should never be used.

SMOKY QUARTZ

placed on the third eye it brings enormous clarity and guidance from the highest source. Petalite forms a guardian angel connection and grounds you during spiritual work—a most useful attribute. Holding a Smoky Quartz or Boji Stone gently brings you back after meditation if you feel "floaty."

How to Meditate with a Crystal

Find a comfortable place to sit, where you will not be disturbed. Hold your crystal in the palm of your hands or put it on a table. Breathe gently and let your attention focus on the crystal. On the out-breath allow any tension you may be feeling to flow through your hands into the crystal where it will be transmuted. On the in-breath feel the transmuted, peaceful energy flowing into your hands. Let the crystal tell you about itself. Feel its qualities. Make them your own by drawing them effortlessly into your body. You may find that you pass instantly into a place of infinite peace, or that you reach this state gradually. Note any guidance that your crystal has for you.

When you are ready to leave the meditation, withdraw your focus from the crystal. Get up and move around.

BELOW If your crystal is too large to hold, place it where your eyes can comfortably rest on it.

LARGE
AMETHYST
POINT

DREAMS

OPAL

MOLDAVITE

Certain crystals induce dreams, and if you see crystals in your dreams, they are trying to speak to you. They may be foretelling the future, offering advice, or warning you about the present.

Crystals such as Dioptase, Emerald, Jade, Ruby, and Moldavite are "stones of inspiration" that generate vivid dreams: pink Moonstone stimulates lucid dreaming. If you slip a Rose Quartz crystal under your pillow, you will dream of your true love. Amethyst or Smoky Quartz protects you against night-mares, while Malachite brings hidden emotions to the surface. Light shining through a crystal in your dreams foretells a speedy resolution to a problem. Hidden jewels guarded by a serpent reveal spiritual treasure in your unconscious mind.

BELOW Placing a Selenite crystal below your pillow can bring insightful dreams.

Crystal Dream Meanings

DIAMONDS	*If you own them in life, slight losses. If not, a small profit.*
JADE	*Prosperity.*
EMERALD	*Good news.*
AMETHYST	*Peace of mind through unexpected good news.*
OPAL	*Great possessions.*
AQUAMARINE	*A happy love life.*
RUBY	*A passionate affair.*
BLOODSTONE	*An unhappy love affair.*
POLISHED AGATE	*Do not be drawn into arguments between friends.*
JET	*Sad news.*
QUARTZ	*Beware being cheated by someone you trust.*
LAPIS LAZULI	*Happy adjustment to circumstances.*
ONYX	*You need advice on an important decision you are delaying.*

Dreaming of Crystal Fish

In a vivid dream, a man brought to me a tray of three crystal fish. I held each one for a long time, marveling at them. I stroked them, seeing how beautiful they were, and watched the colors shimmering as though through ice. The man told me he was going to cook them, which surprised me since I thought they were Fishtail Selenite. When I looked closely, they were alive under the ice. I knew that they were trying to communicate with me.

When I woke I mused on the dream. Fish are a powerful symbol, signifying rebirth—and the psyche swimming in the waters of the unconscious. Encasement in ice signifies something frozen in time. Selenite resonates with the fluids of the body and works on every cell. This could signify a hidden issue needing healing. However, this crystal formed from evaporation of seawater, and water, of course, has been on the planet since the beginning. Selenite facilitates devic contact and holds the information of the ages. This seemed to be something more than a purely personal dream. I instinctively felt that it linked into the evolution of the earth and collective level of consciousness from which dreams arise.

The next morning I was surprised to see a photograph in a newspaper of my three fish, sitting on a dish of ice. I simply had to paint them—a skill I had only recently discovered. As I sat down to paint, I read the caption underneath. These fish were to be genetically modified to make them grow faster—a thought I abhorred.

I programed Fishtail Selenite to send healing to the fish kingdom and asked the devas to help them. As I painted the picture, the fish wanted to make their plight known. The following day, I was asked to write a proposal for this book. I simply had to include my dream of crystal fish!

LEFT Fishtail Selenite is also known as Angel's Wing Selenite. It is a stone with very high vibration.

FISHTAIL SELENITE

CRYSTALS FOR WELL-BEING

Crystals enhance your well-being enormously. Used wisely they can transform your life. They have been used for millennia as a healing tool and to rectify imbalances. Stones such as Peridot enhance your general well-being. Crystals affect the physical, emotional, mental, psychic, and spiritual levels of being. They can overcome stress, encourage you to relax, or stimulate and energize your mind, triggering creativity. They also promote vitality and attract abundance. There are crystals to help you learn and others to enhance your confidence. Some will do both.

Crystals can heal buildings as well as people or pets. Careful siting of a crystal within your home or your workplace can uplift the energies and radically improve your environment. No matter what problems you face, crystals can help. They work at a holistic level: balancing body, psyche, and spirit. Many feelings of physical or mental disease are actually due to energetic disturbance. Crystals radiate good vibrations, so they can gently bring an imbalance back into harmony and restore order to your body or to your psyche. In addition, they can stimulate qualities that are lacking, so they make you feel radiantly whole and able to function more fully.

If you want to attract more joy, infinite support, ample money, and other positive things into your life, then you need crystals for abundance. They help you to manifest a constant flow of all the good things in life.

BELOW Crystals that have been shaped into palm stones are extremely soothing. Blue and Green Fluorite (right and bottom left) and an Amethyst (top left).

HOLISTIC HEALING

MOSS AGATE

Crystals work in an holistic way. They take into account all the different parts of your being—physical, emotional, mental and spiritual—and reach the cause of disease *no matter where it is sited*. As well as relieving symptoms, crystals may also tackle the root of the problem. Your inner state of disease may be at an emotional, mental, or spiritual level, and a crystal will seek this out and redress it.

CRYSTAL HEALING

No one knows quite how crystal healing works. It appears to be through vibration and resonance—after all, our bodies are largely water and water is particularly good at holding vibrational patterns. If your body's vibrational state and your biomagnetic energy field, or aura, have been disturbed or overwhelmed by stronger vibrations such as geopathic stress or environmental "smog" (see pages 72–74), this creates a subtle state of disease which, if not redressed, can ultimately take the form of physical or mental illness. Crystals gently realign patterns and subtle bodies, bringing them back into balance and creating a state of wellness.

THE BODY–MIND EFFECT

Many states of disease mimic, physically, mentally, or emotionally, your state of mind and the feelings you have about yourself or your situation. If you feel "put upon" you develop tension in your shoulders. If you consider yourself unsupported, your lower back goes into spasm. People who worry too much often have overactive intestines or "nervous stomachs."

There is a close link between the mind and the nervous and endocrine systems, as well as between the mind and the emotions. Imbalances in any one will create disturbances in the other three. Correct imbalances and you have perfect health.

USING CRYSTALS FOR HEALING

There are several ways you can use these stones. You can place them on the affected part, or sweep the stones across your body, to pull out disease and realign the subtle bodies. You can also wear a crystal. If you are familiar with meridian-based forms of therapy such as Shiatsu or Acupuncture, you can use crystal wands on meridian points. As long as crystals are not friable, you can put them in your bath. Or, you can make a gem remedy and take this internally and/or bathe the affected part (see pages 50–51 and 99). You can also lay the stones out around your body, or around your bed, so that you are within their energy field.

Some crystals, especially red ones, work very fast—pushing disease out of the body and thereby creating a "healing crisis" in which the condition is exacerbated before it gets better. Other crystals are more gentle. Some work well together in combination: others have conflicting energies. A qualified crystal healer will know exactly the right combination for you.

OPPOSITE Calcite is an energy amplifier, a natural antibiotic and a mental healer so this versatile stone heals holistically.

LARGE GREEN CALCITE

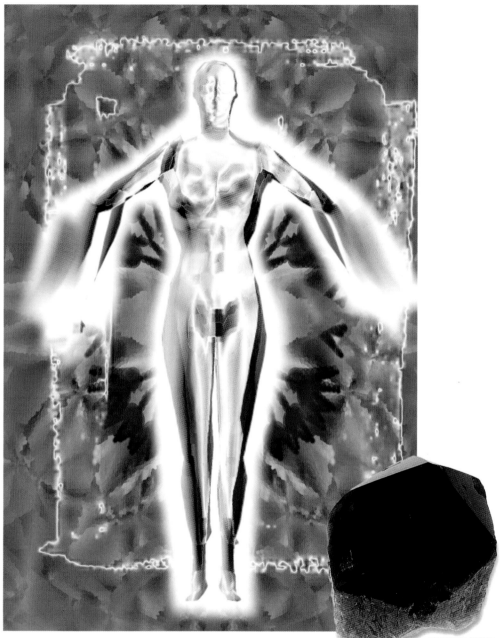

AMETHYST POINT

SELECTING CRYSTALS

Crystals can be selected on the basis of the symptoms you are experiencing, but a much deeper healing takes place if the cause is addressed. Holistic healing takes many factors into account to reach the core problem. If you have several indications and one particular stone keeps cropping up, especially for different levels of the psyche, or if you are strongly attracted to a specific crystal, then this will probably help you. You can also use the stone for your astrological sign. Remember to cleanse and program your crystal first (see pages 16 and 77).

RELIEVING STRESS

ARAGONITE

Stress affects almost everyone at some time in his or her life. It may appear to arise from overwork or life circumstances, but it is rarely as simple as that. The effect of stress may be felt long after the actual trigger is over. For instance, when you appear to be in danger, the adrenal glands go into overdrive and your body is in "fight or flight" mode, which does not necessarily switch off when the danger is past. In this hyped-up state, your body and your emotions are constantly stressed. Crystals gently soothe the body and put you back into a more relaxed mode. By bringing all the parts of yourself, including the subtle bodies that comprise your aura, into balance and harmony, crystals facilitate total healing. Learning to relax also helps you to avoid stress (see page 34).

TUMBLED STONES

If you suffer from stress-related panic attacks, keep a piece of blue-green Smithsonite handy: it gently eases the symptoms, settling your body and calming your fears. It can also heal the root cause of the panic. Keeping a "comforter stone" in your pocket or a handful of "stress relievers"—tumbled crystals that are good for stress—close by can quickly ameliorate potentially stressful situations.

HEALING STRESS

Stress is often based on a mental or emotional attitude. It is a common effect of underlying thoughts such as "I'm not good enough"—an unconscious mental attitude that compels you to push yourself even harder. Such stress leads to overproduction of adrenaline. You become "wired," unable to relax. It can have physical effects such as insomnia and a dysfunctional immune system, but it can also have emotional effects on your relationships and your libido. Crystals work together to tackle this problem at many levels but it is important to ensure that you combine crystals that work together. Certain crystals enable you to relax; others regulate the adrenal glands and the immune system. Yet others will work on your confidence. But some might conflict in their effects.

AQUAMARINE

When choosing your crystals, be sure to find ones that will work in harmony and support each other in their healing work. Palm stones are a tactile way of containing crystal vibes.

CHAROITE

SELENITE

GREEN FLUORITE

So, for instance, if you want to tackle stressed-out adrenal glands, you need a stone that will calm them such as Tiger's Eye. This would also have the effects of giving you some objectivity over the cause of your stressful situation and of calming your nerves. Tiger's Eye also reverses the underlying lack of confidence in yourself and helps you to recognize your inner resources. Aragonite would be a perfect partner for Tiger's Eye. It helps you to be grounded and centered, and can give you insight into the nature of your problem. It can also help you to delegate—taking the pressure off yourself. With your sense of self-worth enhanced, the ability to deal with day-to-day pressures is increased and the stress drops away. Relationships also improve and your mental state is calmer.

Careful choice of supporting stones is essential. If using Tiger's Eye, it would not be beneficial to add Fire Opal to stimulate the immune system or Jade to help you relax because both these crystals also stimulate the adrenals—setting up overproduction of adrenaline once more. Amethyst, however, would support the Tiger's Eye in its work, relieve the insomnia, and promote inner peace.

STRESS RELIEVERS
Amethyst, Tiger's Eye, Sapphire, Aquamarine, Peridot, Aqua Aura, Herkimer Diamond, Amber, Morganite, Aragonite, Calcite, Labradorite, Lepidolite, Aventurine, Lapis Lazuli, Ametrine, Apophyllite, Beryl, Blue Chalcedony, Charoite, Chrysocolla, Larimar, Moss Agate, Rose Quartz, Smoky Quartz, Rhodonite, Serpentine, Selenite, Topaz, Tourmaline

PERIDOT

SAPPHIRE

AVENTURINE
GREEN

AMBER

TIGER'S EYE

CRYSTALS FOR RELAXATION

Crystals create an immensely deep feeling of relaxation. They can be used for mood quietening, centering, and stress reduction. Regular practice of relaxation techniques or meditation can dramatically lower high blood pressure and has many other health benefits in addition to instilling an unshakable sense of well-being.

QUIETENING THE MIND

Playing with crystals is a wonderful way to relax and allow your mind to go out of focus for a while. You can simply let them run through your fingers, or make a crystal mandala. A small bowl of crystals by the telephone calms your thoughts—and stops you from getting too involved with your caller. Using Rhomboid Calcite can take thought away altogether! Crystals can also help you to go into a deep meditative state (see page 25).

RELAXATION

Pink and green crystals induce a deep state of physical relaxation; yellow stones calm the mind, purple stones raise your consciousness and bring peace.

LEFT Keeping a bowl of crystals by the phone helps you to relax and let go.

ABOVE Playing with your crystals induces a deep sense of relaxation. Mandalas have been used to calm the mind for thousands of years.

CRYSTALS FOR RELAXATION

Moonstone, Quartz, Amethyst, Rose Quartz, Smoky Quartz, Citrine, Dioptase, Selenite, Kunzite, Blue Jade, Rhodonite, Chrysoprase, Watermelon Tourmaline, Onyx, Petalite, Kyanite, Rhyolite

RELAXATION LAYOUT

One of the fastest ways to induce deep relaxation is to lay crystals on your body. Quartz induces deep relaxation. A clear Quartz point above your head, pointing downward, draws healing and peace into your aura. Amethyst on your brow quietens your thoughts. Rose Quartz opens your heart, while Citrine, pointing downward from your navel, draws off negative emotions and imparts a feeling of safety. A Smoky Quartz, point down, at your feet draws off negative energy and tension.

Calming Crystals

QUARTZ
Draws in peace and
healing and reenergizes.

AMETHYST
Quietens the
thoughts, relieves
mental tension, and
promotes relaxation.

CITRINE
Draws off negative
emotions and creates
a feeling of safety.

ROSE QUARTZ
Opens the heart to
receive peaceful energy.

SMOKY QUARTZ
Draws off negative
emotions and grounds
the body.

ABOVE You can either position
the crystals yourself, or have a
friend or partner do this for you.
The various types of Quartz have
special roles to play. Leave the
stones in place for at least ten
minutes, preferably longer. You
will feel a different person!

PHYSICAL WELL-BEING

Your physical well-being depends on a number of factors: the state of your body and your mind, how well your immune system is functioning, the surroundings you find yourself in, and your attitude to life. All of these can be enhanced with crystals. Charoite is an extremely useful stone because it transmutes any state of disease into wellness.

CRYSTALS AND THE BODY

Crystals have traditional affinities with the body. Some of these associations arise from the crystals' astrological and planetary connections; others have been discovered through the ancient practice of crystal healing. For example, Amethyst can be placed on the forehead as a traditional treatment for severe headaches. If the pain comes from migraine, Lapis Lazuli is extremely effective. On pages 90–95 in the Crystal Directory you will find a list of specific ailments and stones that can aid them (if your condition is serious, it is wise to consult a qualified crystal healer before embarking on a course of treatment) while on pages 96–97 there is a list of organ correspondences.

CITRINE POINT

LEFT Placing Lapis Lazuli on the forehead provides effective relief from the pain of migraines.

BELOW The zodiac signs have a correspondence with specific parts of the body, and crystals can aid the afflictions to which different signs are prone.

ARIES
Lapis Lazuli heals the headaches to which you are prone.

TAURUS
Aquamarine soothes a sore throat and opens throat chakra.

GEMINI
Chrysocolla aids lungs and nerves.

CANCER
Moonstone aids regulation of menstrual imbalances.

LEO
Magnetite heals lower back pain and aids circulatory system.

VIRGO
Calcite alleviates nervous stomach.

RUBELLITE TOURMALINE
(IN MATRIX)

ENERGY RAISING

One of the fastest ways to enhance your physical well-being is to increase your energy. Yellow and orange stones can raise your energies, but there are many others that will invigorate you. Yellow Jasper is useful if you are suffering from exhaustion—rub gem essence into your skin or put several stones in your bathwater. When you step out of the bath, you will be invigorated.

Crystals for Vitality

APOPHYLLITE	*Natural pyramidal crystals stimulate energy.*
TOPAZ	*Recharges and revitalizes. It is full of warm, vital life-force.*
RUBY	*Amplifies positive energy and creates a pool of restorative energy to draw on.*
CHALCEDONY	*Increases stamina and physical energy.*
AVENTURINE	*Prevents leaching of energy by other people.*
BLOODSTONE	*Increases stamina, balances subtle body.*
CITRINE	*Energizes and invigorates, restores energy resources.*
ORANGE CALCITE	*Maximizes available energy.*
YELLOW JASPER	*Overcomes exhaustion, revitalizes.*
RUTILATED QUARTZ	*Imparts powerful energy when placed on solar plexus.*
DENDRITIC AGATE	*Lessens the energy drain during discordant situations.*
GARNET	*Revitalizes and reenergizes.*
RUBELLITE TOURMALINE	*Activates base chakra and increases physical energy.*

BLOODSTONE

ORANGE CALCITE

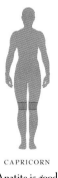

LIBRA	SCORPIO	SAGITTARIUS	CAPRICORN	AQUARIUS	PISCES
Jade is the ultimate healer for kidney problems.	Sardonyx aids elimination when necessary.	Charoite overcomes hip and thigh problems.	Apatite is good for bones and knees.	Amethyst is a powerful healer for all Aquarian ills.	Smoky Quartz is a perfect grounding stone.

THE IMMUNE SYSTEM

BLOODSTONE

An immune system that is compromised leads to all kinds of diseases. If your immune system is not functioning at its peak, it cannot defend you against bacteria, viruses, fungi, and more subtle invaders such as microwaves. Fortunately it is possible to strengthen your immune system with crystal grids or crystal elixirs.

IMMUNE-ENHANCING CRYSTALS

Lying for half an hour with a crystal grid around you, or immersing yourself in a bathtub full of immune-enhancing crystals substantially tunes up your immune system, but it reaches its optimum performance after a night spent with crystals. If your immunity is low, keep the grid permanently in place around your bed, and carry an immune-stimulating stone with you during the day. You may also like to take an appropriate gem remedy, or rub the remedy onto your skin just above your heart where your thymus gland is situated.

Your thymus gland plays an important part in keeping your immune system healthy. Rutilated Quartz and other thymus-stimulating stones can be worn over the thymus (just above the heart) throughout the day.

CRYSTALS FOR THE IMMUNE SYSTEM

Amethyst, Lapis Lazuli, Malachite, Jade, Clear Quartz, Black and Green Tourmaline, Smithsonite, Aquamarine, Azurite with Malachite, Chalcedony, Bloodstone (Heliotrope), Yellow Jasper, Moss Agate, Onyx, Sardonyx, Calcite, Aragonite.

CRYSTALS FOR THE THYMUS

Rutilated Quartz, Aqua Aura, Green Tourmaline, Aventurine, Lapis Lazuli, Dioptase, Clear Quartz.

EMERGENCY IMMUNE STIMULATOR

If you develop an acute infection, immediately place a Bloodstone over your thymus gland and keep it there as long as possible.

LAYING OUT YOUR GRID: SHORT TREATMENT

Make sure you are comfortable before you begin. You can lie on a bed or on the floor for a short treatment. If you do not have any of the crystals mentioned, you can substitute others from the lists.

First of all place Pink Smithsonite over your heart and Green Tourmaline over your thymus (just above your heart). Now place a large Quartz cluster or point above your head (point up). Place eight polished Malachite stones around your body. Leave the stones in place for 30 minutes.

LAYING OUT A GRID: OVERNIGHT TREATMENT

Place Pink Smithsonite crystals by the four corners of your bed and a piece of Smithsonite under your pillow. If you have a large piece of Malachite or Clear Quartz, place this on your bedside table. Tape a piece of Green Tourmaline over your thymus and leave on overnight.

GREEN TOURMALINE

Laying out Your Grid: Short Treatment

QUARTZ

Quartz draws in energy and cleans and revitalizes the physical and subtle bodies. It draws off negative energies.

PINK SMITHSONITE

Pink Smithsonite has powerful healing properties, especially for the immune system.

CHAKRAS AND THE AURA

Chakras are the linkage points between the physical body and the subtle biomagnetic envelope, or aura, that surrounds it. If your chakras are functioning well your whole being is in balance and harmony. If not, you experience physical, emotional, mental, or spiritual disturbance depending on the chakra. The vibration of crystals interacts with your biomagnetic field to bring about healing in the chakras and at all levels.

THE AURA

The aura is the biomagnetic energy field that extends for about 18 inches from the physical body and is made up of several layers pertaining to physical, emotional, mental, and spiritual levels of being. It is visible to psychics, and Kirlian cameras, as a mass of swirling colors, sometimes with darker patches that show energy blockages or depletion in the organs or chakras. Such patches are visible *before* a physical illness manifests.

If the aura is weak, you lack protection against subtle invasion by other people's thoughts and feelings—and illnesses. You could "catch" someone else's headache standing next to the person. Auric depletion almost inevitably corresponds with physical, emotional, or mental disease. With "holes" in your aura, you can be open to psychic vampirism (see page 70–71). Aqua Aura is particularly useful for purifying the aura, and Kyanite aligns the subtle bodies with the chakras.

LEFT The aura is closely related to our physical, emotional, and spiritual state. When the aura is weak, we feel lethargic, tired, and emotional.

ABOVE Aqua Aura cleanses the aura and activates the chakras, creating space for new possibilities to emerge.

The Chakras

Running from the top of the head down the spine (and correspondingly on the front of the body), chakras are energy linkage points between the physical body and your aura. Chakra imbalances can arise when a chakra is too active or overly closed. Crystals bring the chakras back into balance (see Crystal Directory, page 88). Each chakra corresponds to a different color, and stones of that color resonate with the chakra.

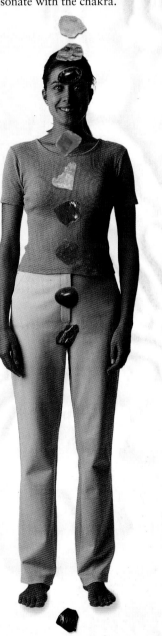

HIGHER CROWN CHAKRAS (white)
Take you into enlightenment and ascension.

CROWN CHAKRA (purple) *Spiritual linkage point. When this opens, you can bliss out. Links to Higher Crown Chakras.*

BROW OR THIRD EYE CHAKRA (indigo) *Linkage point to intuition and other realities. Stuck open, other people's thoughts and feelings rush in. Blocked, confusion takes over and imagination cannot function.*

THROAT CHAKRA (blue) *Point from which you communicate. Blocked, cannot express yourself. Too active, difficult to hear and empathize with other people.*

HIGHER HEART CHAKRA (pink) *Linkage point to universal love. When this chakra opens, relationships move to different level.*

HEART CHAKRA (green) *Allows you to feel and express love. Not functioning, relationships are cold and untrusting. Too open, gullible and too trusting.*

SOLAR PLEXUS (yellow) CHAKRA *Where you feel emotion. Blocked, emotions cannot be expressed. Too open, energy can be leached by others.*

SACRAL (orange) AND BASE (red) CHAKRAS *Creative, sexual chakras. Blocked, libido is low and social interaction difficult. Too active, sexual needs predominate.*

EARTH CHAKRA (brown) *Keeps you grounded and in touch with everyday reality. When not functioning, difficulty in dealing with everyday world. Stuck open, susceptible to adverse earth energies.*

EMOTIONAL WELL-BEING

The psyche is involved in well-being. When your mind, emotions, and spirit are healthy and balanced, you will enjoy a much happier life. Crystals transform energy-sapping emotions, such as worry and fear, and promote positive feelings. They induce a sense of confidence and boost feelings of self-worth. They can also treat the emotional conditions underlying addictions, eating disorders, and fears or phobias.

FINDING EMOTIONAL BALANCE

Crystals access root causes. Malachite draws out deep-seated feelings and clarifies emotions. Aquamarine helps you to understand the cause of your emotional disease and Green Fluorite dissipates emotional trauma. If you have been thrown off balance emotionally, crystals will restore your equilibrium. Sodalite and Rhodochrosite create emotional balance. Use stones in healing layouts or wear them on your person: Emerald, Sapphire, and Diamond are excellent emotional balancers. If you have been unable to let go of painful feelings, Rose Quartz and Blue Lace Agate gently cleanse and neutralize the resulting toxicity. Rose Quartz also helps you avoid emotional overreaction, as does Moonstone. If you feel emotionally scattered—or shattered—Amethyst and Opal balance your

ROSE QUARTZ

ROSE QUARTZ
One of the best all-round emotional healers, Rose Quartz cleanses, detoxifies, and soothes. It lifts depression, encourages self-acceptance, and aids forgiveness.

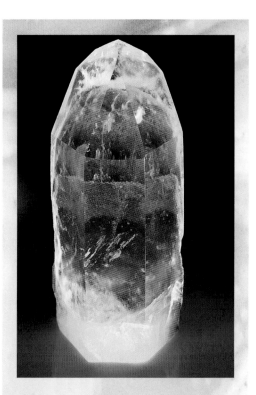

Landscape Quartz

The crystal to which you are attracted will often tell your story. This one shows a troubled childhood at the base and difficult early adulthood healed through years of therapy. At the point where the crystal clears, the owner's mother died and she was released into a new life. The phantom and the rainbow toward the top point the way to happiness and spiritual evolution.

emotions and bring you more control. If worry is ruining your life, Petalite gently transforms this into trust and inner security.

Emotional disease may stem from events in childhood or be more recent in origin. Old hurts must be mended before you feel comfortable in an adult relationship (see page 66). Crystals go back to the source of the pain and gently dissolve it. Rhyolite, for instance, helps you to process the past and enhances your self-esteem, while Fluorite opens the gate to the subconscious mind.

HEALING THE CHILD WITHIN

Smithsonite, with its powerful connection to the child within, is an excellent emotional healer. The pink form soothes the emotional body and gently releases deep-seated childhood trauma; the blue-green form releases and transmutes anger and rage. Yellow Smithsonite works on the solar plexus and mental body where emotional wounds and nonproductive attitudes are stored. Once these are released, your body–mind produces a sense of well-being.

Wonderfully blue and uplifting, Larimar works on the inner child at a higher vibration. It links to the angelic inner child: a perfect

being full of playfulness and joy. Activating this energy heals the traumatized child within and releases fear. Larimar promotes the shedding of cleansing tears and heals heart-trauma. This stone removes self-constraints, dissolves sacrificial behavior, and helps you to take control of life.

HEALING DEPRESSION

Depression is a debilitating disease. Its causes are many and varied, but the holistic nature of crystal healing means that emotional equilibrium can be restored with the aid of Amber, Citrine, Jet, Chrysolite, Smoky or Rose Quartz. Sardonyx lifts depression. If you swing between depression and elation, Kunzite stablizes you. Moss Agate deals with depression caused by left–right brain imbalances. Yellow Apatite treats lethargy and depression. Anger often underlies depression, and Agate or Peridot neutralize destructive, bitter anger while Kyanite dispels frustration. Red Jade helps you in the constructive expression of justifiable anger, and Chalcedony dispels hostility and ensures you will be heard.

BLUE-GREEN
SMITHSONITE

PINK SMITHSONITE

LARIMAR

GUILT AND FORGIVENESS

Guilt underlies many states of disease. Chrysocolla heals guilt and fear, and enables you to speak your truth. One of the quickest and most effective ways of healing emotional disease is to forgive yourself and anyone else involved. Rhodochrosite, Rose Quartz, Selenite, and Chrysoberyl aid this process and are supported by Celestite, which replaces negative feelings with self-empowering love.

CONFIDENCE

Having confidence in yourself together with a strong sense of self-worth can transform negative emotions. Chrysocolla enhances personal confidence. Chalcedony removes self-doubt and shows you your true worth. Hematite boosts low self-esteem, while Tiger's Eye links you to inner resources that underlie self-confidence. Muscovite dispels insecurity and self-doubt. If you need strength of will, Rutilated Quartz brings this together with quiet confidence and the ability to make decisions. Green Tourmaline allows you to avoid situations that bring up self-doubt and negativity before you become entangled in them. If you need to know your life path, Sodalite, Quartz, Topaz, Selenite, and Mahogany Obsidian show you the way.

Alleviating Crystals

ADDICTIONS	Amethyst, Kunzite.
PHOBIAS AND FEARS	Aquamarine, Aventurine, Green Calcite, Chrysoprase, Kunzite, Iron Pyrite, Tourmaline, Obsidian with Rhodochrosite or Rose Quartz.
EATING DISORDERS	Danburite; Anorexia: Rose Quartz, Topaz; Bulimia: Yellow Apatite, Lapis Lazuli.
STABILIZE	Kunzite, Rose Quartz.
MOOD SHIFTS	Amazonite, Chrysocolla, Hawk's Eye, Turquoise, Serpentine.
JEALOUSY	Peridot, Chrysanthemum Stone.
OBSESSION	Green Jasper.
STUCK FEELINGS	Apache Tear.
BITTERNESS	Agate.

AMAZONITE

IRON PYRITE

CHRYSOCOLLA

MENTAL WELL-BEING

GOLDEN BERYL

Crystals can help to overcome mental stress and restore intellectual equilibrium. They fortify memory and concentration, improve your ability to learn, increase your creativity, and rectify inefficient mental strategies. Crystals can also be used to help regulate mental disease and to dispel confusion.

MENTAL EQUILIBRIUM

If you are one of those people whose head is always buzzing, crystals can help you to calm your thoughts. If close-mindedness is a problem, Blue Chalcedony gently opens the mind and aids in assimilating new ideas; Fluorite does the same for narrow-mindedness. Amethyst is a very powerful mental healer, making you feel less scattered and more in control mentally. This crystal actually aids neural transmission of information and boosts your memory. It also helps you to focus on realistic goals and facilitates your body's ability to act on information from your mind. An Amethyst layout is excellent for creating mental calm and equilibrium.

Rhomboid Calcite and Blue Selenite shut down thought, bringing absolute mental peace, while Apophyllite balances excessive mental energy in your head. Placing one of these stones on or above your head, or touching it to your third eye quickly creates equilibrium but you can also wear appropriate crystals in your ears or around your neck for longer-term effects.

If you suffer from persistent mental pressure, holding an appropriate crystal gives relief. Keeping a suitable stone on your

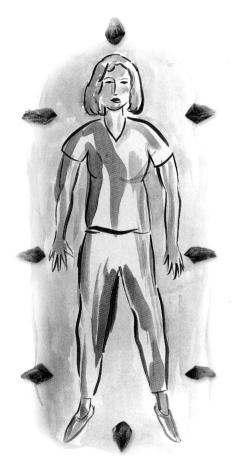

ABOVE Placing eight Amethyst points around your body brings relaxation and mental equilibrium.

desk is helpful, putting one in the bath when you get home from work quickly shuts off thoughts of your day. Green Jade focuses your thoughts onto what is important, allowing other thoughts to drift away. Aquamarine filters out unimportant information, increasing clarity and preventing mental overload. Beryl filters out distractions and teaches you to ignore what is unnecessary while at the same time sharpening intellect for the task in hand.

45

CHRYOSPRASE

RHODOCHROSITE

ONYX

UNPOLISHED
SAPPHIRE

KUNZITE

DIOPTASE

HEALING THE MIND

If your mental stress has reached serious proportions, Dioptase and Green Calcite are powerful mental healers and can prevent mental breakdown, as can Rhodochrosite. This crystal attunes you to your higher self, removes any denial, and aids you in integrating new concepts and information. It restructures your mind in the process. Beryl clears the mind, inducing tranquillity and focused thoughtfulness.

If psychiatric disorders need attention, try Chryosprase, which has been used for hundreds of years to heal mental disturbance. It calms and opens the mind to new experiences. Kunzite actually contains lithium—used in psychiatry to control bi-polar disorders. It is extremely useful taken as an elixir (see pages 50–51). It aids you in adjusting to pressure and shields you from any undue mental influence from another person. Blue Obsidian brings mental clarity and can aid in schizophrenia, Alzheimer's, and multiple personality disorder. A Quartz Elestial crystal can also aid schizophrenia. It stabilizes brain wave frequencies and disperses confused thoughts. Chalcedony helps dementia and senility. Carnelian gently dispels delusions, and Lapis Lazuli dissolves hallucinations.

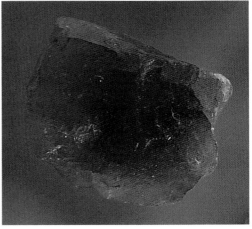

DANBURITE

CRYSTALS TO AID CONCENTRATION

Agate, Yellow Apatite, Fluorite, Citrine, Sapphire, Aragonite, Hematite, Amethyst, Lepidolite, Onyx, Smoky Quartz, Rhyolite, Black Tourmaline, Danburite.

CRYSTALS FOR IMPROVING MEMORY

Green Calcite, Opal, Amber, Azurite, Hematite, Citrine, Yellow Fluorite, Amethyst.

CRYSTALS FOR LEARNING

Golden Calcite, Amethyst, Blue Chalcedony (aids learning foreign languages), Fluorite (all colors), Danburite.

OVERCOMING LEARNING DIFFICULTIES

Sugilite (Luvulite) is an excellent stone for working with learning difficulties such as dyslexia and for autism. It aids mental coordination and softens the challenges being faced. Purple Sapphire also aids dyslexia. A Diamond can encourage logical thought and stabilize a chaotic mind. A less expensive option is a Fluorite crystal, which dissolves fixed ideas and aids the organizational side of the brain and the ability to cross-reference information. It also stimulates the absorption of new information. Blue Obsidian addresses speech difficulties, and Blue Chalcedony improves verbal dexterity. Yellow Apatite overcomes lack of concentration and inefficient learning strategies.

RIGHT **Wearing** Turquoise earrings is an excellent way to improve your creative problem-solving abilities.

GOLDEN CALCITE

OPAL

DIAMOND

AMBER

RHYOLITE

AMETHYST

CRYSTAL GRIDS

CHAROITE

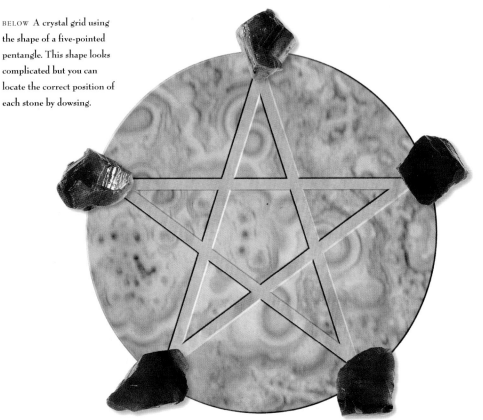

Crystal grids protect your well-being, enhance your energies, and help you sleep at night. They enhance your confidence and memory, or attract love. They can be laid out with large, chunky crystals, but small polished stones often work just as well.

SETTING OUT YOUR GRID

There are two ways of setting out a grid. The simplest method is to put a stone in each corner of the room or to place them around your bed. There is also a more metaphysical method, which involves dowsing to see exactly where each stone should be placed—and in what order. This may involve a complex geometric shape such as a five-pointed pentangle, but you do not need to know how to draw such a shape. Simply moving a crystal around the bed until the pendulum changes direction will be enough to show you the order in which to place the stones (see How to Dowse on page 49). Choose stones that are appropriate for your purpose. If you want to aid your memory, for instance, uses pieces of Green Calcite; if you need to make decisions, Charoite will help you; if you have flu or some other acute infection, Bloodstone will help alleviate it.

BELOW A crystal grid using the shape of a five-pointed pentangle. This shape looks complicated but you can locate the correct position of each stone by dowsing.

NIGHTTIME GRID FOR INSOMNIA

If your insomnia is caused by geopathic or electromagnetic stress, that is, you feel wired and jittery for no apparent reason, a grid of Herkimer Diamonds around your bed will protect you and facilitate an excellent night's sleep. Large Herkimer Diamonds work well. They are not as pretty as the smaller, clear stones, but they have a powerful effect. Most Herkimers are double terminated, in which case place them parallel to the bed. Quartz points can be substituted; place them point-out to deflect energies. You will need at least five stones, maybe more—dowse for this.

Program the stones to bring you peaceful sleep. Place one stone on each side of the bed just below your shoulders. Place two more stones level with your hips (check with a pendulum for exact position). Finally place one at the end of the bed.

RIGHT Small Herkimer Diamonds are bright and clear. Larger Herkimers have oily traces and dark patches.

HERKIMER DIAMOND

How to Dowse

When setting out your grid, dowsing will help you to decide where to place your crystals, and in which order you need to place them.

DOWSING

To dowse for the right spot you will need a crystal on a chain (a pendulum). Clear Quartz is ideal. Hold the chain between your thumb and fingers with about a hand's width of chain hanging down. It should feel comfortable.

CHECK "YES" OR "NO"

To check for "yes" and "no," hold the pendulum over your hand. State your name and ask if that is correct. The crystal will swing in a particular way. This is "yes." Then state another name and ask if this is your name. The crystal will swing in a different way to indicate "no."

TO PLACE A CRYSTAL

To place a crystal in your home, draw a sketch map of the room, ask where the right place is, and move the pendulum until you get a "yes." Alternatively, place the crystal in different parts of the room and check its position with the swing of the pendulum.

GEM ELIXIRS

TOPAZ

One of the most powerful ways of absorbing crystal vibrations is by the use of gem remedies, or elixirs. Purpose-made ones can be bought, but it is easy to make your own.

VIBRATIONAL MEDICINES

Because crystals have such powerful vibrations they are ideal for making an energy medicine that works on the body, mind, emotions, and spirit. Water takes on the vibrational pattern of a substance placed within it, and then passes it on by absorption into the body via the lining of the mouth or through the skin. It resonates with any disharmony, gently realigning the subtle energies that created disease. It can also help negate "invaders."

PURPLE FLUORITE

Viruses, for example, are impossible to kill with conventional medicine but Fluorite essence has powerful antiviral properties.

Vibrational medicines have been around for thousands of years. Water that had been in contact with crystals or plants was used as far back as the time of ancient Egypt for bathing or as an internal medicine. In the Middle Ages, the nun Hildegard of Bingen used many recipes for gem elixirs, including Topaz for the eyes.

MALACHITE

USING GEM ELIXIRS

Gem essences can be taken internally by mouth, dropped onto the skin, or bathed in. If you make a gem essence that is purely water, store it in the refrigerator and use within a week. You can either put two teaspoonfuls into a glass of water and sip throughout the day, or put 6 drops into a dropper bottle of spring water to administer a few drops every 15 minutes in acute cases, or three times a day for less severe conditions. You can also bathe the affected part or add the elixir to your bathwater. If the gem essence is made from a toxic crystal such as Malachite or is for balancing chakras, put some on your hands and pass them around your body about a foot away.

If you use at least 50 percent brandy or vodka as a preservative, the essence will last much longer, especially since you can use this "mother tincture" to make a dosage bottle. Fill a dosage bottle with a mix of one quarter brandy (unless applying to the eyes) and three quarters water, add a few drops of elixir, and shake the bottle. In acute cases, take one drop every few minutes.

If you are using your gem essence to cleanse a room—Black Tourmaline is an ideal stone for this—you should put a few drops into clean water in a mister or spray bottle. (Use vodka as a preservative.) You can also spray Citrine Elixir to clear your mind and improve your concentration (see the Crystal Directory for more elixirs and their effects).

Gem remedies are an ideal way to treat pets. Put a few drops in their drinking water or their food. Alternatively, place some on your hands as you stroke them.

Making Gem Elixirs

Making your own gem elixirs is a satisfying process. You can store them for personal use later, or give them away as presents.

Select and cleanse your crystal.

Pour pure spring water into a clean glass bowl.

Place the crystal in the water.

Leave in the sun for twelve hours.

Bottle in a clean glass bottle, preferably dark glass, with an air-tight stopper.

Add at least 50 percent brandy if you wish to keep the essence for more than a week.

Store the elixir in a cold, dark place, properly labeled and dated.

Add to your bath or use to make dosage bottles or sprays.

Always dilute well with pure spring water before applying to the skin or eyes.

Remember

Always cleanse a crystal before making an elixir (see page 77).

Never use a toxic stone such as Malachite unpolished. Polished stone elixirs from toxic crystals should be used only for external application.

Dark colored glass protects the energies of the essence better than clear.

To preserve an elixir use a minimum of 50 percent brandy or vodka.

CRYSTALS IN THE HOME

DENDRITIC
AGATE

The power of crystals balances and enriches your living space. Careful positioning of crystals can improve the ambience of the rooms in your home. You may wish to create a calm, safe atmosphere for times when you are alone. On social occasions you might want to use the crystals to energize a room so that it is welcoming to guests. Where you place crystals can also have an impact on other areas of your life. They can be used to enhance your career prospects or your wealth, to attract helpful friends, or even to make your houseplants grow better.

BELOW Placing a crystal in your plant pots is not only decorative, it can aid their growth, prolong flowering, and keep them healthy.

BELOW Some crystals can fade in strong sunlight and others could well focus strong rays, causing a fire. Opaque crystals such as Black Tourmaline are the most appropriate choice for a windowsill but clear Quartz can be used with care.

ABOVE Placing a crystal on a light box brings out its beauty and radiates energy.

TRANSFORM YOUR ENVIRONMENT

To transform the energies in your home, you could, for instance, hang a faceted Quartz crystal in the window and watch as a myriad rainbows magically light up the space. Placing a crystal on a light box has the same effect. Placing a beautiful and decorative Chrysanthemum Stone in a prominent place exudes calm confidence and brings your endeavors to fruition.

CHRYSANTHEMUM STONE

53

ENHANCING AMBIENCE

Because crystals radiate energy out into a room, you can use them to create a calm and peaceful space, or to energize and activate. If you are looking for a safe haven after a busy day, a large Amethyst cluster, geode, or single point radiates tranquility. Place it close to your favorite chair. Turquoise brings in wisdom, aiding you in the search for your true self. The pure white of Selenite exudes serenity and quietens the mind—and brings the angelic realms closer, as do Celestite and Angelite. Rose Quartz or Kunzite in your bedroom puts you in the mood for love. Petalite creates a protective, grounded spiritual space—keeping one in your car protects against accidents.

TURQUOISE

If you want to give your place a buzz for a party, try using a stimulating Red or Orange Calcite, or a clear Quartz cluster. If it's creativity you are after, placing a large piece of Lapis Lazuli or Amazonite close to your desk or easel fires the imagination. You can encourage your plants to grow by popping a piece of Dendritic Agate into their pots. To protect yourself from the emanations of a computer or other electromagnetic devices, place a piece of Lepidolite or Fluorite on top.

ABOVE Gem stones are often used to fashion decorative objects such as this turquoise Kuau Yin, goddess of wisdom and compassion.

BELOW Red Calcite can make your party go with a swing—it ignites passion.

RED CALCITE

CRYSTALS AND FENG SHUI

CLEAR QUARTZ

In the ancient Chinese art of Feng Shui different parts of the house, or of a room, reflect different areas of your life. Placing appropriate crystals in a specific place can powerfully transform the aspect of your life that corresponds to that spatial area. It is particularly auspicious to place a crystal in both the part of the house and the section of the room that are related. The easiest system to use is centered on the front door (or the door by which you usually enter). The crystals should be as large as possible and should be cleansed regularly.

Auspicious Crystals

A Citrine geode generates wealth and helps you hold on to it. The stability of a large Agate geode imparts confidence and aids your business success and fame. Rose Quartz attracts love into your life, and Dravide Tourmaline heals the family line. Clear Quartz generates health and well-being. Lapis Lazuli stimulates your creativity. Malachite attracts helpful friends, while Amber is beneficial and protective, manifesting exactly the right circumstances for your fulfillment and career advancement. Apatite stimulates both intellect and spiritual seeking, taking you to the highest knowledge.

CITRINE GEODE
Wealth

AGATE GEODE
Fame

ROSE QUARTZ
Relationships

DRAVIDE TOURMALINE
Family/Ancestors

CLEAR QUARTZ
Health and well-being

LAPIS LAZULI
Creativity

APATITE
Learning/knowledge

AMBER
Career

MALACHITE
Helpful friends

door

CRYSTALS IN THE WORKPLACE

BLACK
TOURMALINE

Crystals also help to enhance your working environment and to improve relations with your colleagues. There are crystals to aid problem-solving, improve communication, and help you deal with your day-to-day experiences.

ENHANCING THE WORKING ENVIRONMENT

All the stones that create a less stressful atmosphere such as Amethyst, Rose Quartz, Sugilite, Smoky Quartz, and Kunzite will enhance the environment of your workplace. Place one on your desk or in a drawer, tape it under a table, or put it discreetly in a corner—crystals will work even when hidden behind a filing cabinet. You can also wear one under your clothes or keep it in your pocket. However, most people instinctively respond to the good vibes a crystal puts out, and, since they are highly decorative objects, a crystal in the workplace will most likely be admired. It can also be useful to keep a small bowl of polished stones around—either for yourself or for other people to play with. Their soothing properties will soon make themselves felt!

If you are in a job where complaints or even abuse are possible, keep a Black Tourmaline close to you—you can tape one to your phone if necessary. Jet and Sardonyx both turn away violence, and Rose Quartz and Sugilite bring in a more loving energy.

SODALITE

TEAMWORK

If you work as part of a team, Yellow Fluorite supports cooperation between members of that team, as does Emerald, while Tiger's Eye aids in reaching your goals. A Smoky Quartz draws off any negative energies and Pink Chalcedony helps to resolve any conflict. Other crystals that resolve conflict are Jasper, Lapis Lazuli, Rhodonite, and Sugilite. If communication is a problem, especially where there is bickering or criticism, try placing Aquamarine or Sodalite in the room— you could tape it under a table if you meet around one. Sodalite is useful for changing attitudes. If you find it difficult to express your ideas to your colleagues, wear a Sapphire. If taking constructive criticism is difficult for you, a Citrine will allow you to be open to this. Where compromise is needed, Serpentine facilitates it.

REDRESSING MISSING QUALITIES

Crystals can build in qualities that are necessary for your work. Apatite promotes a humanitarian attitude and service. If enthusiasm for your job is lacking, put a Carnelian in your pocket. If you need to heighten your motivation, make that crystal a Topaz or wear Apatite. To develop your leadership skills, use Apatite or Ruby, to enhance self-expression use Kyanite. Kyanite is also useful when you need a strong voice. Fluorite aids concentration, and if you need a clear and focused mind, Selenite is the stone for you.

SOOTHING TIRED EYES

Bathing with an elixir soothes eyestrain and aching eyes. Keep some elixir (well diluted in water) in a dropper bottle and remember to put 2 or 3 drops into your eyes at regular intervals.

LAPIDOLITE

FLUORITE

SUITABLE EYE ELIXIRS:

Topaz, Jadeite, Aquamarine, or Blue Lace Agate

PROBLEM-SOLVING

Crystals help you combine analysis with an intuitive solution. They help you to see things from a new perspective and activate hidden talents.

BELOW Lepidolite, Fluorite, or Black Tourmaline prevent electromagnetic stress from computers and TVs.

Problem-Solving Crystals

GREEN TOURMALINE *Aids lateral thinking, analyzing difficulties, finding a conclusion.*

AQUAMARINE *Filters unnecessary information, helps concentrate on the essence of the problem.*

APATITE *Interface between consciousness and matter, stimulates manifestation, brings about a result.*

AMAZONITE *Combines intellect and intuition, fires creative process.*

PERIDOT *Highlights essence of problem.*

OBSIDIAN *Brings up hidden factor (use circumspectly).*

AZURITE *Brings action on problems.*

RUTILATED QUARTZ *Gets to the root cause and overcomes resistance to innovative solutions.*

TOURMALINATED QUARTZ *Dissolves crystallized patterns, harmonizes disparate elements.*

TURQUOISE *Harnesses creative energy, shows where you fit in.*

CHROSOPRASE *Draws out unrecognized talents.*

MUSCOVITE *Dispels insecurities and aids intuitive problem solving.*

CRYSTALS FOR ABUNDANCE

Everyone dreams of wealth and prosperity. But abundance is so much more than this. It is also about attracting joy, support, nurturing, creativity, plenitude, and love into your life, allowing you to expand as well as manifesting everything you need. Abundance is limitless, effortless, and trusting.

BOUNTEOUS ENERGY
The bounteous energy of crystals enables you joyfully to attract into your life all that you need to support your well-being. Abundance brings prosperity of spirit rather than purely material goods. However, there is no reason why a fabulous house or car should not be on your abundance program!

TIGER'S EYE GANESH,
HINDU GOD OF WEALTH

To magnetize abundance into your life, first select your crystal. Yellow crystals are strongly connected to prosperity. If you need to meet helpful people, or have material desires, Tiger's Eye or Hawk's Eye can help you. A Yellow Sapphire worn touching your finger can attract wealth, while Citrine in your cashbox brings prosperity. Topaz taps into your own natural resources and unlocks your philanthropic side. It teaches you that when you give, you open yourself to receive. Dendritic Agate is traditionally known as the "Stone of Plenitude." It is excellent if you are growing any kind of crop but it also stimulates abundance and fullness of life.

ABUNDANCE CRYSTAL **One**
long Quartz crystal with
many tiny ones at the base
attracts abundance
and well-being.

TOPAZ

HAWK'S EYE

YELLOW
SAPPHIRE

ABUNDANCE CRYSTAL

WEALTH		
	FRONT DOOR	

ABOVE You can combine crystal placement with the Chinese system of Feng Shui to gain wealth. Divide up your home or a room into sections as shown to locate your Wealth Corner and place a suitable crystal in it.

THE WEALTH CORNER

In the Chinese system of Feng Shui, the farthest left-hand corner from the entrance is your Wealth Corner. Crystals to place here include a huge chunk of Citrine—a cluster or a geode—or an Abundance Crystal. An Abundance Crystal is a large Clear Quartz crystal with masses of tiny crystals at its base. (If your bathroom is located here, remember to keep the door shut and the toilet seat down, otherwise whatever wealth you attract will simply "go down the pan." Standing a geode here reverses the effect, as does Ruby, which helps you to hold on to your wealth.)

In addition to the house's Wealth Corner, each room in your house also has a Wealth Point. This is located on the farthest left point from the door. Placing a Hawk's Eye in the Wealth Point of each room draws helpful people and material goods into your life.

CARRYING ABUNDANCE WITH YOU

Programing a crystal for abundance and carrying it in your pocket constantly reminds you that you are drawing plenitude toward you. Carnelian is especially useful for this.

It helps you to help yourself, improves your motivation, and gets you out of a rut. When programing, use a positive affirmation such as "I constantly attract abundance, prosperity, and joy into my life." Repeat this statement whenever you hold the stone.

CRYSTALS FOR ABUNDANCE
Tiger's Eye, Yellow Sapphire, Hawk's Eye, Quartz, Carnelian, Topaz, Peridot, Dendritic Agate, Citrine, Diamond, Bloodstone, Moonstone, Moss Agate, Red Garnet, Ruby

PERIDOT

CARNELIAN

CITRINE GEODE
A geode helps you to hold onto your wealth as well as attracting more.

CRYSTALS IN LOVE

Using crystals is a wonderful way to bring more love into your life. Whether it's revitalizing an existing relationship or attracting that dream lover, there is a crystal to help. Crystals radiate love at many levels. You may be looking for physical passion, or seeking a soulmate with whom to have a soul union. Some crystals take you to a high spiritual love vibration while others are earthy and libidinous.

With a myriad of crystals to choose from be sure to make the right selection. Confusing Jasper, which ignites sexual passion and prolongs pleasure, with a more spiritually attuned crystal such as Rhodochrosite may bring you empathetic love but not necessarily the passion you were seeking. Combination stones can be useful. Green Tourmaline brings on the action, and Pink Tourmaline releases your inhibitions. Put the two together and you have Watermelon Tourmaline.

Being able to give and receive love depends on so many factors. If you have old hurts or are caught up in the past, new loves will be affected. If you are unable to love and accept yourself, it is difficult to accept love from someone else. If your heart has been broken, it needs to be healed before you find intimacy again. Fortunately crystals come to the rescue here. They gently dissolve such blockages to love.

If your heart chakra is open, you will be much more open to receive love. There are many crystals that heal and stimulate this point. Place a crystal over your heart and allow it to do its work. Love will do the rest.

BELOW Stones of love and passion: Rhodochrosite and Red Jasper, Rose Quartz, and Amethyst.

RHODOCHROSITE

RED JASPER

ATTRACTING A LOVER

ROSE QUARTZ

SUGILITE

Crystals can help you to find a soulmate or even a quick fling; they can symbolize eternal union, or kindle instant passion. Place a piece of Rose Quartz by your bed and it will enhance existing relationships or attract new ones.

FINDING LOVE

If you are looking for love, slip Rose Quartz under your pillow or place a large piece by your bed—it is so effective you may need to add an Amethyst to calm things down! This stone has an amazing ability to radiate love—and to attract it. (It is used in the Crystal Love Ritual on page 15.) If you are a person of mature years, Green Aventurine or Rhodochrosite have the same effect. If you are seeking love but are not sure that you want commitment, avoid Magnetite. This stone quickly attracts the one for you—but in olden times it was used to test a wife's fidelity. A husband would secretly place it under his wife's pillow. If she fell out of bed in the night, she was no longer virtuous!

It will help to program the crystal to bring exactly the right lover for you—remember to state that he or she must be available, free, and ready for love and commitment if these are important to you.

RIGHT A Soulmate, or Tantric Twin crystal, has two same-sized crystals side by side and springing from the same base.

If you are looking for a true soulmate, someone with whom you can share your deepest thoughts and feelings, find yourself a Soulmate crystal or a beautiful piece of Sugilite. This stone is also called Luvulite and is known as the Love Stone. It connects you on a very deep soul level. If you are looking for love in the material realm, Rubellite Tourmaline is the answer.

SOULMATE
CRYSTAL

CRYSTALS FOR ENGAGEMENT RINGS

For her: Diamond: bonds relationship; Green Sapphire: ensures loyalty and fidelity; Emerald: promotes domestic bliss and successful love; Red Garnet: represents enduring love; Opal: fosters passion; Morganite (Pink Beryl): attracts and retains love. For him: Sardonyx: long-lasting happiness in marriage.

RIGHT The stones in an engagement ring all have powers of their own and particular meanings. It is important to consider these when choosing a ring.

SOULMATE CRYSTALS

Soulmate crystals, or Tantric Twins, are a pair of crystals approximately the same size growing from a common base, joined together along one side but with distinct and separate terminations. Tantric means "union of

energies." These stones have a powerful message concerning the bonding of two people into a close and intimate relationship. They teach how to be unique and separate, and in equal partnership. To be in a successful union, you need to be comfortable with yourself. If not, you will project your unresolved issues onto your partner. Tantric Twins help you to know and accept yourself truly. As a result, interdependence and deep intimacy with another person are possible.

If you are fortunate enough to find a Tantric Twin Quartz crystal that has vivid rainbows across the intersection, then your relationship will be particularly harmonious. You will find a true soulmate. Place your Soulmate crystal in the relationship corner of your house or bedroom—the farthest right from the door.

TAKING A CRYSTAL LOVE BATH

A crystal bath is a wonderful way to experience crystal love and to attract a lover or deepen a relationship you already have. Simply cleanse a suitable love crystal such as Rose Quartz or polished Pink Beryl (Kunzite is too delicate and would be better made into a gem elixir) and place it in your bath. If you want to rekindle passion, try Carnelian, Garnet, Fluorite, or Ruby; for a spiritual soulmate, Rhodochrosite; for mature love, Green Aventurine. As you soak, absorb the energies. Ideally, share the bath with your partner. At night, slip the stone underneath your pillow.

REVITALIZE YOUR RELATIONSHIP

UNPOLISHED
RUBY

If you are in a long-term relationship, it may be feeling stale. You may need to rekindle passion or find a deeper intimacy. Crystals can quickly revitalize the relationship and help to sort out any difficulties. They can heighten libido, communication, and intimacy, resolve conflict, and also help to make your bedroom a much sexier place. Simply place a chunk of the appropriate stone by your bed or pop a smaller piece under both pillows. Wearing Red Garnet jewelry will revitalize your feelings and enhance your sexuality.

Revitalizing Crystals

VARISCITE

FLUORITE *Rekindles libido.*

AMAZONITE AND VARISCITE *Help to overcome impotence.*

JASPER *Prolongs sexual pleasure—also brings problems to light before they cause difficulties.*

CHIASTOLITE

RED GARNET OR RUBY *Revitalizes feelings, enhances sexuality.*

PINK OR RUBELLITE TOURMALINE *Aphrodisiac, releases inhibitions.*

GREEN TOURMALINE *Increases the action. Watermelon Tourmaline combines the two.*

SERPENTINE *Opens a pathway for the kundalini to rise (see page 65).*

TOURMALINATED QUARTZ *Revives deadened feelings.*

MUSCOVITE *Dissolves feelings of uncertainty, opens the heart to intimacy.*

GREEN JADE *Improves dysfunctional relationships.*

SUGILITE (LUVULITE) *Fosters forgiveness and love.*

OPAL *Brings stability to a relationship.*

CHIASTOLITE *Transmutes conflict into harmony.*

CITRINE *Resolves money worries.*

TURQUOISE *Unites male and female, aids in understanding each other.*

SMITHSONITE *Heals the inner child, opens to intimacy.*

JADE *Brings harmony, increases love.*

RHODOCHROSITE *Stimulates selfless love and compassion, aids emotional expression.*

DIAMOND *Bonds relationships.*

EMERALD *Induces domestic bliss and loyalty.*

MUSCOVITE

TOURMALINATED
QUARTZ

TURQUOISE

ENHANCING LIBIDO

Red and orange crystals are particularly useful for firing up the libido. Lack of libido is often due to blockages in the lower chakras. Crystals can quickly dissolve these blockages, allowing sexual energy to rise up the spine, inducing a supercosmic orgasm.

LIBIDO LAYOUT

This layout can be a joyful shared experience between you and your partner, but you can ask a friend to place the stones. Lie on the floor or on the bed. Ask your partner to place the stones slowly and with reverence and joy. This is a gift he or she is giving to you. Together you are honoring your sexual energy. *Have your partner place the Quartz points around your body, points out. The Serpentine goes between your legs and the red stone at the base of your pubic bone. The orange stone sits just below your navel, with the yellow stone at your solar plexus. The green stone is placed on your heart. Allow any feelings to rise up into consciousness without judgment. Acknowledge them and wait until they fade.*

You will feel the kundalini energy rise up your spine from your base chakra. Allow this rise to intensify until your whole spine is on fire. Finally, the Rose Quartz or Kunzite goes at the top of your head. Feel love radiating down through the Rose Quartz, meeting the kundalini force and pervading your whole body. At this point, your partner will no doubt want to take a more active part in the proceedings.

If you or your partner suffer from impotence, add Amazonite or Variscite to the layout. Place them at the base chakra.

You will need:
6 Clear Quartz Points,
1 Serpentine, 1 Red
Sardonyx, Red Jasper,
or Red Calcite,
1 Orange Calcite or
Orange Carnelian,
1 Yellow Citrine or
Yellow Jasper,
1 Green Amazonite,
Chrysoprase, or Green
Tourmaline, 1 Rose
Quartz or Kunzite.

HEALING PAST HURTS

RAINBOW
OBSIDIAN

AGATE

If you are holding on to past hurts or suffering from the effects of abuse, it will be difficult to give or receive love. Rose Quartz, Kunzite, and Purple Tourmaline are the great heart-healers. They gently release blockages and promote love, but other crystals will heal conditions that prevent you from loving fully.

LARIMAR

Emotional Healing Crystals

ROSE QUARTZ *Gently dissolves the cause of a broken or hurt heart and brings peace to the heart, opening to universal love.*

KUNZITE *Removes emotional debris from past relationships.*

LAVENDER JADE *Heals those who have been hurt by love in the past, bringing gentleness.*

PINK SMITHSONITE *Heals abandonment, rejection, and abuse; rebuilds trust.*

PURPLE TOURMALINE *Produces loving consciousness, connects base and heart chakras, healing abuse and allowing sexual energy to flow freely.*

BLUE QUARTZ *Overcomes fear of reaching out to others.*

PINK PETALITE *Heals the heart meridian, releases past hurt.*

ANGELITE *Transmutes pain and disorder into wholeness and healing.*

BLUE-GREEN SMITHSONITE *Heals emotional wounds and inner child.*

RAINBOW OBSIDIAN *Cuts the cords of old love, releases hooks from heart.*

PINK TOURMALINE *Reassures it is safe to love again—including oneself.*

AGATE *Overcomes bitterness of the heart and eliminates inner anger.*

CHRYSOCOLLA *Heals heartache, increases capacity to love.*

RHODOCHROSITE *Helps heart to assimilate painful feelings without shutting down.*

APACHE TEAR *Relieves grievances. Releases unshed tears, bringing insights into pain and creating acceptance and healing of one's wounds.*

RHODONITE *Nurtures love and heals trauma.*

MALACHITE *Breaks unwanted ties and outworn patterns.*

LARIMAR *Dissolves sacrificial behavior, radiates love and peace.*

OBSIDIAN *Cleanses the heart of outgrown ties and painful memories.*

LAVENDER
JADE

RHODONITE

ANGELITE

OPENING THE HEART CHAKRA

DIOPTASE

RMELON
MALINE

With your Heart chakra fully awakened and functioning perfectly, you will be open to give and to receive love. An open and trusting heart is one of the greatest gifts that you can bring to a relationship.

HEART CHAKRA LAYOUT

Placing crystals over your heart opens, balances, and energizes your Heart chakra. An unbalanced heart leads to cold, "heartless," power-seeking relationships or to overly responsible, self-sacrificing, "victim" interaction. A balanced heart chakra, on the other hand, leads to life-enhancing, interdependent union. Watermelon Tourmaline is known as the Super Activator for the Heart. It brings together the green of the heart chakra with the pink of love. Rubellite or Red Tourmaline stimulates loving consciousness. You can augment the heart chakra layout by placing a large piece of Rubellite nearby.

In addition to your Heart chakra, there is also the Higher Heart chakra located a little above the heart. This too can be activated by crystals such as the wonderful blue-green Dioptase, which allows you to access the higher dimensions of love.

BLUE QUARTZ

CRYSTALS FOR THE HEART CHAKRA

Kunzite, Green Sapphire, Ruby, Peridot, Green Quartz, Rose Quartz, Morganite (Pink Beryl), Muscovite, Green Tourmaline, Watermelon Tourmaline, Blue Lace Agate, Chrysocolla, Lepidolite, Chrysoprase, Pink Danburite, Pink Petalite, Green Aventurine. Higher Heart: Dioptase, Kunzite, Kyanite.

BELOW Place 7 Rose Quartz, 1 Dioptase, and 1 Watermelon Tourmaline as shown and leave in place for 20 minutes. Four Amethyst points can be added, point facing outward, to draw off any emotional imbalances that may be blocking the heart.

ROSE QUARTZ OR KUNZITE

AMETHYST

DIOPTASE

WATERMELON TOURMALINE

67

CRYSTALS TO PROTECT

Since time immemorial crystals have been used for protection. Ancient people carried amulets and talismans to keep them safe. The dead were buried with crystals to ensure a safe onward journey. Curses were turned aside, gods invoked to defend personal and communal space, and earth energies were regulated by the power of crystals. Nowadays geopathic stress and electromagnetic pollution are on the increase and many people find themselves caught up in "sick building syndrome." The energy disturbances these create can be overcome by the right use of stones.

People today are still affected by "ill-wishing" just as they were in olden times. Other people are jealous, have negative thoughts, or become angry and utter curses. They seldom stop to think about the effect. But your energy field will sense those thoughts like daggers. Fortunately, crystals can protect you—and may return ill-wishing to its source so that the perpetrator can understand the harm he or she is doing. You may also come under "undue influence." A friend, colleague, or parent with a strong mind can coerce you to act and think in the way they want. Wearing a crystal cuts through that influence and keeps you safe.

If you live in a neighborhood where there is crime, you can protect your home with a few well-placed crystals. Jet, for instance, protects against violence. If you have disturbingly noisy neighbors, positioning a large piece of Rose Quartz against the wall nearest to them magically calms and quietens the atmosphere.

UNPOLISHED JET

RIGHT Jet has been used for centuries as a protector.
FAR RIGHT Clear Quartz, Black Tourmaline, and Iron Pyrite are a powerful protective combination in this crystal cluster.

POLISHED

PROTECTING YOURSELF
AND YOUR AURA

When your aura is functioning correctly, it screens out other people's thoughts and feelings, prevents energy loss, and provides a barrier against environmental influences. Crystals strengthen and protect your aura and turn back any negative energies.

MAINTAINING A STRONG AURA
Your aura marks out "your space." If someone stands too close, you feel uncomfortable because his or her aura is penetrating yours. An aura weakened by illness, energy depletion, psychic attack, or emotional or mental pain appears to have "holes" or to billow out into space. These disturbances let other people's thoughts and feelings through—and leave you open to energy depletion.

BELOW Slipping an Apache Tear into your pocket turns away negative energies. Wearing Labradorite has the same effect.

APACHE
TEAR

LABRADORITE

Holding a Quartz crystal in front of your solar plexus instantly doubles the size and strength of your aura, and Quartz can be used to detect and repair "holes." Labradorite and Apache Tear protect your aura from negative energy. Wear Labradorite jewelry or slip an Apache Tear into your pocket (see also The Crystal Directory, page 88).

A psychic vampire is someone who feeds off other people's energy. If you feel tired after you have been with a friend or colleague, it is possible that you could have been vampirized. Aventurine and Labradorite are the crystals that protect against this. If vampirism comes from someone with ill-intent, Black Tourmaline is the crystal to use.

DOUBLE
TERMINATED
QUARTZ

REPAIRING AURIC HOLES
You can locate and repair holes in your aura using crystals. With your eyes closed, slowly run an Amethyst or Quartz point over your body (or ask a friend or a partner to do this for you). An auric hole will feel cold and energyless. Leave the crystal over the hole for a few moments, with the point facing inward to your body. It will become warm and energized once more. Continue this process until the whole aura has been healed.

CRYSTALS FOR REPAIRING THE AURA
Holes: Amethyst, Carnelian, Citrine, Quartz
Detaching Mental Influence: Selenite, Kunzite
Releasing Negativity: Aqua Aura
Aligning Chakras and Aura: Kyanite

ILL-WISHING

The aura can be influenced by ill-wishing. At its most extreme this becomes psychic attack: a situation in which a person deliberately wishes you harm. You can protect yourself by wearing an appropriate crystal such as the highly effective Black Tourmaline, Ametrine, Amber, or Fire Agate. Black Tourmaline with Mica and Fire Agate return ill-wishing so that the source can understand the effect of their actions. Place a crystal by your front door or wear it around your neck. You may also find yourself under undue influence from a strong mind. This may be deliberate or you may unconsciously act on someone else's thoughts. Selenite and Kunzite deal with this, while Pyrolusite dispels interference from

BLACK TOURMALINE WITH MICA

ABOVE Black Tourmaline comes in several forms. Combined with Mica, it is particularly useful for warding off ill-wishing or electromagnetic pollution.

BLACK TOURMALINE CRYSTAL

the psychical or spiritual world. "Comb" your aura with the crystals, or wear them around your neck or as earrings.

CREATING A PROTECTIVE CRYSTAL

Hold an appropriate crystal in your hands for a few moments, visualizing its powers of protection surrounding you. Place the crystal in a spiral and wear around your neck.

CRYSTALS FOR PERSONAL PROTECTION

To attract a guardian angel: Celestite or Angelite
To connect to divine protection: Amethyst
To create a psychic shield: Black Tourmaline, Ametrine, Aventurine, Labradorite
To draw off negative energy: Apache Tear

LEFT Wearing a Carnelian gives you the protection of a strong aura, as does Amber jewelry, which also attracts abundance.

71

PROTECTING YOUR SPACE

Keeping good vibes in the space around you is vital if you are to enjoy good health on all levels. Clean environmental and auric energy are as important as clean water.

GEOPATHIC STRESS

The Earth has its own subtle energy field and meridians (called ley lines). If the earth's grid is disturbed, creating geopathic stress, there is a disturbance in the energies of people living on ley lines. This commonly results in energy depletion and a compromised immune system.

Several factors contribute to geopathic stress: underground water; the natural water table—if this rises the incidence of geopathic stress increases; underground nuclear weapons testing—shock waves travel thousands of miles; and emanations from underground pipes and cables that adversely affect the Earth's grid. You may need to call in a dowser or Earth energy healer, but moving your bed from an area of geomagnetic stress and blocking its effect with crystals can also be beneficial.

CRYSTALS FOR GEOPATHIC STRESS

Large pieces of Kunzite, Amethyst, Obsidian, Apache Tear, Black Tourmaline, Fluorite, Clear and Smoky Quartz, Turquoise, Herkimer Diamond, Larimar, Aragonite. (Dowse for the right crystal and appropriate placement, see page 49)

ENVIRONMENTAL SMOG

The air is filled with invisible smog, composed of electromagnetic emanations, microwaves, radio and infrared waves, and radar radiation. In the home, smog is created by televisions, computers, microwave ovens, and telephones, even when appliances are switched off. (To protect yourself from your computer, put Lepidolite or Fluorite on it.) Whenever you step outside your home you are likely to be assaulted by microwaves from mobile phones or masts. (If you use a mobile phone, tape a piece of Black Tourmaline to it.) You may be affected by high-voltage electricity or nuclear radiation. Your working environment may include high-energy technology.

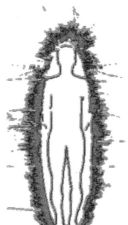

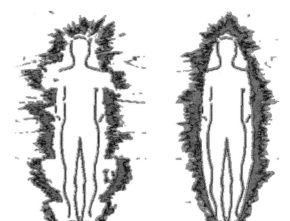

LEFT **Aura of woman. Note 'hole' by the ear she puts her mobile phone to. (Phone is off but damage visible).**

CENTER **Aura of same woman one minute later with mobile phone switched on 10 feet away.**

RIGHT **Aura of same woman using mobile phone fitted with Black Tourmaline crystal**

ABOVE Placing a Smoky
Quartz or Black Tourmaline
between yourself and
pylons protects you from
electromagnetic emanations.

BELOW Wearing a Black
Tourmaline means that you
are protected at all times
from environmental smog.

Although manufacturers assure us that
the electromagnetic dosage is safe, there are
serious doubts about this especially when
the effect is cumulative and you are already
geopathically stressed. Doctors and dowsers
have found that people whose energy fields are
adversely affected by mobile phone masts are
inevitably geopathically stressed as well.

A Kirlian camera takes pictures of the
energy field surrounding the body. Simply
holding a mobile phone that is switched
on but not connected can dramatically
disintegrate your auric field—as does standing
next to someone who is using one. This effect
is reversed by an appropriate crystal. Apache
Tear, Black Tourmaline with Amazonite, and
very large diamonds are particularly effective.

If you are suffering from geopathic stress
and environmental pollution, use Obsidian
to block the energies and wear an Apache
Tear to protect yourself. However, a word
of warning, Obsidian brings shadow energies
to the surface for dispersal. If you are not
ready to face these, choose another stone
such as Amethyst or Smoky Quartz.

CRYSTALS FOR ELECTROMAGNETIC POLLUTION

*Black Tourmaline,
especially when
combined with
Amazonite, Lepidolite,
Fluorite, Green or
Brown Jasper, very large
Diamonds, Obsidian,
Sodalite, Malachite, Herkimer
Diamond, Yellow Kunzite,
Turquoise, Jet. (Wear small
stones or place large ones
between yourself and the
source of the pollution or
lay out a grid, see
pages 38 and 75.)*

BOJI STONES
MALE (LEFT)
FEMALE (RIGHT)

PROTECTING YOUR HOME

Placing a Black Tourmaline outside your front door deflects negative energies and deters burglars. An Amethyst geode or large cluster gives all-round protection. A Sardonyx grid around the house in areas of high population protects from crime. Laying out a Selenite grid affords spiritual protection and a skillfully programed Clear Quartz acts as an efficient ghost-buster.

A SAFE WORKING SPACE

Clear Quartz dispels the static electricity that is often found in offices and that contributes to sick-building syndrome—a state where the energies in a building are so bad they create disease amongst the occupants. A large Smoky Quartz creates a protective bubble that keeps you free from other people's stress and frustration. If your own job is stressful, keep a piece of Rose Quartz or Amethyst handy and hold this whenever you can. It will calm your energies and disperse them safely. Wearing an Aquamarine has the same effect. Remember to clean the crystals regularly. (See page 77.)

PROTECTING YOUR CAR

Jet has been used for centuries to protect against violence. Programing a piece of jet and leaving it in your car defends you against road rage and your car against damage—accidental or deliberate—as will Sardonyx and Petalite.

DISPERSING AND GROUNDING NEGATIVE ENERGY

Negative energy can arise from the space itself, and what has happened there, or it may be created by depressed thoughts, aggression, or confusion. You feel dragged down in its presence. If allowed to remain, it can create physical, mental, or emotional disease.

Black stones and Smoky Quartz absorb negative energy, which can then be replaced by positive energy from a bright crystal. Some stones, such as Jade, release negative thoughts, and Ametrine breaks debilitating emotional patterns. Clear Petalite renders negative energy impotent.

Without your feet firmly on the ground and your subtle bodies aligned, you are more open to picking up negative energies and to invasion by other people's or environmental energies. Earthy colors ground energy, so brown, gray, and green crystals are particularly good at grounding you. If you feel uncomfortable with your surroundings, hold a Carnelian, which is strongly attuned to Earth and yet uplifts the spirit.

CRYSTALS FOR DISPERSING NEGATIVE ENERGY

Kyanite, Smoky Quartz, Green Calcite, Chalcedony, Jade, Jet, Apache Tear, Citrine, Amber, Kunzite, Chiastolite, Malachite, Pyrolusite, Aragonite

CRYSTALS FOR GROUNDING

Agate, Boji Stone, Carnelian, Green Fluorite, Hematite, Amber, Brown Jade, Jasper, Onyx, Smoky Quartz, Snowflake Obsidian, Charoite

PYROLUSITE

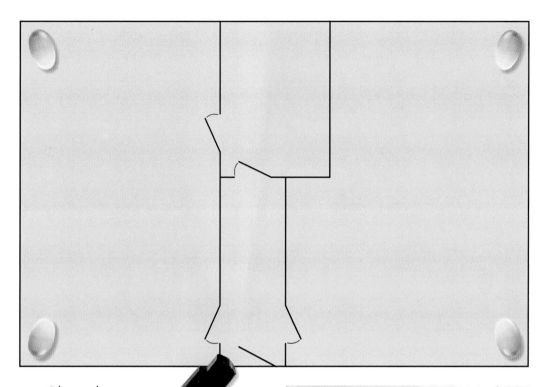

ABOVE Selenite grids create spiritual protection for your home and a Black Tourmaline protects against electromagnetic stress and burglars.

BLACK TOURMALINE

LAYING OUT A PROTECTIVE GRID

Crystal grids protect a bed, a room, or the whole building. Large chunky crystals work well and look decorative, but you can choose smaller, discreet crystals such as polished Selenite or unpolished gemstones such as Ruby. Use appropriate stones that have been cleansed and programed to do their work. Place a stone at or in each corner (for a building put them outside if possible; if not, place one at each of the outer corners).

POLISHED
SELENITE

Crystals for Grids

AGAINST PSYCHIC ATTACK *Black Tourmaline, Ruby, Kunzite.*

AGAINST PSYCHIC INTRUSION *Selenite, Kunzite, Pyrolusite.*

AGAINST ENERGY LEACHING *Aventurine.*

AGAINST ELECTROMAGNETIC OR GEOPATHIC STRESS *See list on page 73.*

TO AID INSOMNIA OR TO PROTECT YOUR BED *Herkimer Diamond, Amethyst, Lepidolite, Labradorite.*

FOR PROTECTION DURING SPIRITUAL WORK OR MEDITATION *Selenite, Labradorite, Lapis Lazuli, Azeztulite.*

AGAINST THE POSSIBILITY OF VIOLENCE OR CRIME *Jet, Sardonyx.*

TO CALM NOISY NEIGHBORS OR PROMOTE PEACE IN THE HOUSE *Rose Quartz, Kyanite.*

TO ALLEVIATE FEAR *Rhodochrosite.*

CRYSTAL CARE

APOPHYLLITE

Crystals need to be looked after. They respond to loving, nurturing care. If you treat your crystals with respect, then they in turn will serve you well. Crystals tend to absorb negative vibrations very easily, so it is important that you cleanse your crystals regularly. This ensures that their energies remain high and their power continues to be effective. You may also need need to recharge them from time to time.

CARING FOR YOUR CRYSTALS
Although some crystals, such as clear Quartz and the grainy darker crystals, are able to withstand light, crystal colors will become faded after prolonged exposure to sunlight. To allow your crystals to continue to look their best, make sure that you position them away from the direct sunlight of windows or keep them covered when they are not in use. Wrapping delicate crystals carefully in a soft cloth or placing them in a cloth bag ensures that they are not scratched or chipped—it is important to keep soft and hard crystals separate so that the harder ones cannot damage the softer ones. If you include a Carnelian, it will help to cleanse the stones. Some crystals are affected by damp, which can penetrate between layers or separate points from a larger cluster. It is essential to keep all crystals free from dust and dirt.

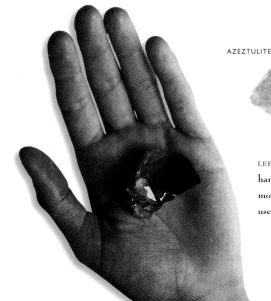

AZEZTULITE

CARNELIAN

LEFT Stones that are handled frequently need more cleaning than those used for decoration.

ABOVE Azeztulite is one of the few stones that never need cleaning. Carnelian can clean other stones.

CITRINE CLUSTER

CLEANSING

Citrine, Kyanite, and Azeztulite are self-cleaning but all other crystals need to be regularly cleansed. Some stones, such as Carnelian or Quartz, have the capacity to purify other crystals. Cleansing is especially important if you have only just received your crystal or if you are using it for protection or healing.

There are several methods of cleansing. Choose the one that is right for your crystal. Most tumbled stones and single crystal points are happy being washed under flowing water, but soft, friable crystals or mica-based ones should never be immersed in water and this can harm clusters too. Selenite is water-soluble and will eventually disappear if washed. When cleansing crystals, hold a strong intention that all negative energies will be transmuted and the crystal will be reenergized and ready for use again.

BELOW Many crystals are suitable for cleansing in water, others in salt. Salt can also be added to water.

ABOVE Holding crystals under running water gives an instant clean.

CLEANSING WITH WATER

If you live close to the ocean, you can take advantage of your natural surroundings and immerse suitable crystals in seawater (placing them in a washing basket or mesh bag) for an hour or two. After they have soaked in the seawater, the crystals will need to be rinsed in pure water. If you do not live near to the ocean, putting a handful of sea salt in a bowl of water works equally well. Crystals can also be held under running water for a few moments. Make sure you allow them to dry naturally in the sun.

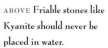

ABOVE Friable stones like Kyanite should never be placed in water.

QUARTZ CLUSTER

A Quartz or Citrine cluster, or an Amethyst geode can be used to clean some smaller stones. Place the stone you wish to clean on the cluster and leave it there for a period of about 12 hours. Standing this arangement in sunlight or moonlight can also reenergize the crystal at the same time.

LIGHT VISUALIZATION

You can rapidly cleanse a crystal by passing it through light. You can also use light visualization. Simply visualize a column of pure golden light falling on the crystal. Concentrate on holding this thought in your

BELOW Placing small stones on a large Quartz cluster purifies and then reenergizes them.

mind's eye as the light cleanses and transmutes the energies in your crystal. (If you find it difficult to use the visualization technique, you can achieve the same results by holding the crystal in front of a candle flame.)

SALT

Friable stones can be placed in a bowl of dry salt and left overnight. It is essential that you thoroughly remove any excess salt from the crystal afterward since it could absorb damp from the atmosphere and damage the surface of the crystal.

ABOVE Passing crystals through light is an excellent way to cleanse them.

RIGHT Friable crystals can be placed in salt—which must be thoroughly brushed off afterward.

SMUDGING

The smoke from smudge or joss sticks quickly cleanses crystal energies. Hold the crystal in the smoke for a few minutes.

CRYSTAL CLEAR

It is also possible to purchase a purpose-made crystal cleanser. *Crystal Clear* is a highly effective brand. Allow a few drops to fall on the crystal, or drop them into the washing water. You can also spray them from an atomizer to clean all crystals, or the environment, instantly (atomized spray is gentle and does not damage delicate crystals, see www.sacredsites.co.uk/sites/petaltone.)

RECHARGING

Sunlight is an excellent reenergizer for crystals—as is the moon for Moonstones or Hematite. However, it is best to avoid the hot midday sun because rays focused through a clear crystal can cause burns. Sunrise is an excellent time for using this methed as it concentrates the purifying and invigorating energy directly into the crystal.

LEFT Spray bottles or Crystal Clear are useful for misting crystals or a room.

ABOVE Polished stones can be kept together in a bag but more delicate or easily scratched stones should be kept separately to avoid damage. If you do keep your crystals in a bag, put them in the sunshine from time to time to reenergize them.

THE CRYSTAL ZODIAC

Each of the 12 signs of the zodiac has special crystal affinities. Some arise from your month of birth, others from the planets connected to your sign. Most crystal connections go back thousands of years but fresh links are made as consciousness expands and new crystals come to light. As crystals are found, they are assigned an astrological connection.

Other crystals are associated with the "rulership" of your sign. This is the planet that resonates most strongly with your sign. So, for instance, Mars, named after the brash God of War, rules the pushy and assertive sign of Aries, the first sign of the zodiac. In medieval astrology, Mars also ruled Scorpio, a powerful but much more reserved sign. With the discovery of Pluto, rulership of secretive Scorpio was assigned to this enigmatic planet. (The god Pluto always wore his helmet of invisibility when he came up from the Underworld.) The old rulership was not lost, so Scorpio has affinities with both martian and plutonian stones. Martian Ruby is the birthstone of Aries and also has strong affinities with Scorpio, while plutonian Malachite is a Scorpio birthstone. Malachite is most appropriate to the depths and intensity of Scorpio, being a Stone of Transformation.

BELOW Cancer is ruled by the Moon as are its birthstones: Pearls and Moonstone.

Birthstones ground and amplify celestial energies. Wearing your birthstone harnesses the power of your specific crystal. Using other stones attracts beneficial vibrations, balances less desirable tendencies, or enhances innate potential. All enrich your life and help you to become more *yourself*.

RUBY

DIAMOND

ARIES
March 21 to April 19

KEYNOTES Energetic, assertive, confident, ebullient, egocentric, passionate.

BIRTHSTONES Ruby, Diamond.

AFFINITIES Amethyst, Aquamarine, Aventurine, Bloodstone, Carnelian, Citrine, Diamond, Fire Agate, Garnet, Jadeite, Jasper, Kunzite, Magnetite, Pink Tourmaline, Orange Spinel, Ruby, Topaz.

As an Aries you are assertive, pushy, strong minded, and "me oriented." Wearing a Diamond will help you to become more "other oriented" and considerate of the needs and feelings of the people around you. You have drive and courage, and you often act impetuously. Your birthstone, the passionate and intense Ruby, has to be handled with care. It can explosively bring feelings and emotions to the surface—such as anger—and you may need to balance it out with a Carnelian to avoid finding yourself in dangerous situations. Kunzite brings out a more gentle side of the passionate love that as an Aries you so readily express.

TAURUS
April 20 to May 20

KEYNOTES Reliable, methodical, loyal, practical, productive, stubborn, creative.

BIRTHSTONES Emerald, Topaz.

AFFINITIES Aquamarine, Azurite, Black Spinel, Boji Stone, Diamond, Emerald, Kunzite, Kyanite, Lapis Lazuli, Malachite, Rhodonite, Rose Quartz, Sapphire, Selenite, Tiger's Eye, Topaz, Tourmaline, Variscite.

While outwardly a sensible soul, inwardly you have the sensuousness and hedonism that your ruler, voluptuous Venus, bestows. Wearing her stone, the Emerald, helps you to find successful love and an outlet for your sensuality. Yours is a practical, earthy sign, and the intense midnight blue of Lapis Lazuli encourages you to raise your eyes to the heavens, opening your intuitive side and taking you beyond the material world. Taureans are noted for their resistance to change, and Peridot is the stone par excellence for facilitating necessary change.

BLUE TOPAZ

EMERALD

GREEN TOURMALINE

PINK AGATE

CANCER
June 21 to July 22

KEYNOTES Sensitive, protective, moody, ambitious, sympathetic, nurturing.

BIRTHSTONES Moonstone, Pearl.

AFFINITIES Amber, Beryl, Brown Spinel, Calcite, Carnelian, Chalcedony, Chrysoprase, Emerald, Moonstone, Opal, Pink Tourmaline, Rhodonite, Ruby.

As a moon-ruled sign, you are prone to mood swings. Moonstone keeps you balanced and helps you take time for inward reflection. It assists you to understand your emotions and inner vulnerability, and to harness your intuition and apply it practically. (You may need to remove Moonstone at full moon.) Your sign has a tendency to be possessive, and Moonstone's ability to keep close to you that which is dear may need to be offset by Rhodonite's expression of unconditional love. Pink Tourmaline lets go of the past, moving you forward.

GEMINI
May 21 to June 20

KEYNOTES Adaptable, communicative, quick, light-hearted, sociable, dual, changeable.

BIRTHSTONES Tourmaline, Agate.

AFFINITIES Apatite, Apophyllite, Aquamarine, Blue Spinel, Calcite, Chrysocolla, Chrysoprase, Citrine, Dendritic Agate, Green Obsidian, Green Tourmaline, Sapphire, Serpentine, Rutilated and Tourmalinated Quartz, Tiger's Eye, Topaz, Variscite.

Gemini people are always on the go. You have an innate ability to multitask that is aided by your Agate birthstone. This stone enables you to pay precise attention to details while still seeing the bigger picture and avoiding nervous tension. Your affinity with the stone of truth, Apophyllite, overcomes a tendency to be economical with the truth and to disregard inconvenient facts. A Tourmaline birthstone is particularly appropriate for such a dual sign: it balances the two sides of the brain and integrates your inner and outer selves.

MOONSTONE

PEARL

LEO
July 23 to August 22

KEYNOTES Dramatic, open, regal, proud, generous, playful, bossy.

BIRTHSTONES Cat's or Tiger's Eye, Ruby.

AFFINITIES Amber, Boji Stone, Carnelian, Cat's Eye, Chrysocolla, Citrine, Danburite, Emerald, Fire Agate, Garnet, Golden Beryl, Green and Pink Tourmaline, Kunzite, Larimar, Muscovite, Onyx, Orange Calcite, Petalite, Pyrolusite, Quartz, Red Obsidian, Rhodochrosite, Ruby, Topaz, Turquoise, Yellow Spinel.

Leo is hard to miss, and the flamboyance of Cat's Eye appeals to you, as do all the golden stones associated with your sign. Like them, you radiate benevolent warmth—until someone upsets your dignity. Kunzite aids humility, and Topaz overcomes injured pride and restores your usual sunny self. With its ability to overcome limitations, it also helps you gain the recognition you crave. Use it to develop your creative potential. As you belong to a sign with a tendency to play hard, Topaz is useful. It overcomes exhaustion, revitalizing your energy.

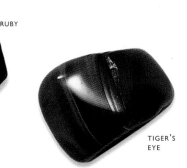

RUBY

TIGER'S EYE

PERIDOT

SARDONYX

VIRGO
August 23 to September 22

KEYNOTES Analytic, modest, discriminating, efficient, critical, creative.

BIRTHSTONES Peridot, Sardonyx.

AFFINITIES Amazonite, Amber, Blue Topaz, Dioptase, Carnelian, Chrysocolla, Citrine, Garnet, Magnetite, Moonstone, Moss Agate, Opal, Peridot, Purple Obsidian, Rubellite, Rutilated Quartz, Sapphire, Sardonyx, Smithsonite, Sodalite, Sugilite.

Virgo is a sign that values truth and virtuous conduct, and your birthstone, Sardonyx, resonates to these qualities. Sardonyx also assists you in finding a stable relationship and attracts friends into your life. Peridot, your second birthstone, has the ability to get to the nub of the matter. It also assists in letting go of detrimental habits that block your growth. As a Virgo, you have a tendency to seek perfection, and while Amber attunes you to universal perfection, Rubellite (Pink-Red Tourmaline) overcomes your tendency to be too critical of yourself and of others.

LIBRA
September 23 to October 22

KEYNOTES Diplomatic, adaptive, harmonious, cooperative, partnership-led.

BIRTHSTONES Sapphire, Opal.

AFFINITIES Ametrine, Apophyllite, Aquamarine, Aventurine, Bloodstone, Chiastolite, Chrysolite, Emerald, Green Spinel, Green Tourmaline, Jade, Kunzite, Lapis Lazuli, Lepidolite, Mahogany Obsidian, Moonstone, Opal, Peridot, Sapphire, Topaz.

Relationships are extremely important to you, and you may be tempted to choose an Opal ring to signify faithfulness in love. A Sapphire might be appropriate since this brings dreams to fruition, together with lightness and joy. Opal amplifies traits, bringing them up so that you achieve the perfection you seek. Opal also stimulates your creativity and releases your inhibitions. Your sign has a tendency to be judgmental. Aquamarine overcomes this. Mahogany Obsidian helps you achieve your aspirations, removing blockages to your life's work.

OPAL

SAPPHIRE

MALACHITE

TOPAZ

SCORPIO
October 23 to November 21

KEYNOTES Intense, deep, magnetic, powerful, secretive, sexual.

BIRTHSTONES Topaz, Malachite.

AFFINITIES Apache Tear, Aquamarine, Beryl, Boji Stone, Charoite, Dioptase, Emerald, Garnet, Green Tourmaline, Herkimer Diamond, Hiddenite, Kunzite, Malachite, Moonstone, Obsidian, Red Spinel, Rhodochrosite, Ruby, Topaz, Turquoise, Variscite.

Yours is an intense and magnetic personality. You are not afraid to penetrate the taboo areas of life. Your Malachite birthstone is a stone of transformation that aids you in your journey. Its qualities of loyalty and fidelity resonate strongly with you. Your emotions run deep, and Malachite aids you in understanding and releasing experiences that cause you disease or distress. Scorpio has a tendency to hold on to resentment, and your other birthstone, Topaz, helps you to forgive and let go.

TURQUOISE

BLUE TOPAZ

CAPRICORN
December 22 to January 19

KEYNOTES Careful, ambitious, controlled, responsible, disciplined, organized.

BIRTHSTONES Jet, Onyx.

AFFINITIES Amber, Aragonite, Azurite, Carnelian, Fluorite, Garnet, Green and Black Tourmaline, Jet, Labradorite, Magnetite, Malachite, Onyx, Peridot, Quartz, Ruby, Smoky Quartz, Turquoise.

Yours is a serious sign, enlivened by a strong sense of humor. Your birthstone, Onyx, provides the structure and authority you desire and strengthens your confidence. Labradorite aids feeling comfortable with your strong sense of duty and destiny. The "New Age" stone Apatite helps you to find perfect harmony within yourself and facilitates development of your powerful but often overlooked intuition. It can link you to spiritual masters, transferring their knowledge into your consciousness. This gives you the spiritual authority you seek.

SAGITTARIUS
November 22 to December 21

KEYNOTES Optimistic, questioning, adventurous, freedom-loving, tactless.

BIRTHSTONES Topaz, Turquoise.

AFFINITIES Amethyst, Azurite, Blue Lace Agate, Chalcedony, Charoite, Dark Blue Spinel, Dioptase, Garnet, Gold Sheen Obsidian, Labradorite, Lapis Lazuli, Malachite, Pink Tourmaline, Ruby, Smoky Quartz, Snowflake Obsidian, Spinel, Sodalite, Turquoise.

Your birthstone, Topaz, is an excellent companion on your eternal quest for knowledge. For you, traveling is more fun that arriving, and Topaz broadens your perspective and lights your path. Your other birthstone, Turquoise, protects you and helps you to attune to unseen realms. It acts as a guide to the unknown and brings spiritual peace. As a Sagittarian you tend to live in the future. Charoite helps you to stay in the present moment and to find the gift in all that you encounter.

JET

ONYX

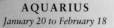

AMETHYST

AQUAMARINE

PISCES
February 19 to March 20

KEYNOTES Fluid, emotional, intangible, vacillating, malleable, artistic.

BIRTHSTONES Moonstone, Amethyst.

AFFINITIES Aquamarine, Beryl, Bloodstone, Blue Lace Agate, Calcite, Chrysoprase, Fluorite, Labradorite, Moonstone, Smithsonite, Turquoise.

Pisces moves fluidly between two worlds: everyday reality and the psychic planes. Labradorite and Amethyst form a bridge. Highly intuitive and sensitive, you need your birthstone, Amethyst, to protect and cleanse your energies. It gives you the boundaries you find difficult to develop. Your other birthstone, Moonstone, resonates with your intuitive nature and helps you to apply spiritual insights to the everyday world. It, together with Blue Smithsonite, aids in releasing emotional blockages and keeps your body and emotions in balance.

AQUARIUS
January 20 to February 18

KEYNOTES Unconventional, independent, idealistic, humanitarian, far-sighted.

BIRTHSTONES Aquamarine, Amethyst.

AFFINITIES Amber, Amethyst, Angelite, Antacamite, Aquamarine, Blue Celestite, Blue Obsidian, Boji Stone, Chrysoprase, Fluorite, Labradorite, Magnetite, Moonstone.

You are always ahead of the trends, and Amethyst supports the assimilation of new ideas. It aids you in finding ways to put your vision for the future into practice now. Boji Stones resonate to a cause dear to your heart: the brotherhood of humanity. Universal truths are also important to you, and Aquamarine instills these. Belonging to a fixed and yet highly unconventional sign, it is easy for you to move out of balance. Angelite and Blue Celestite realign you, while Magnetite counteracts nervous tension and increases your tolerance of emotional pressures.

AMETHYST

MOONSTONE

CRYSTAL DIRECTORY

Crystals can be used for a multiplicity of purposes and their qualities are many and varied—as are their colors and forms. If you need to identify a crystal or ascertain its qualities, you can do so in the pages that follow. If you require a crystal for a specific purpose, the Directory will help you to find the appropriate stone.

The Crystal Directory is laid out in sections. A list of stones for specific ailments and conditions is on pages 92–95, together with gem remedies and their effects on page 99. There is a diagram of the chakras on page 96, followed by body diagrams to enable you to identify an organ and the crystals that aid it on page 97. Crystals for the aura are laid out on page 98.

The guide to Crystals goes from clear, brilliant gemstones—rarely so bright in their unfaceted form—through clear crystals into opaque stones. If you need to identify a crystal, look at it closely. Is it rough and grainy? Or faceted and bright? Does it have points? Natural facets and points are usually found on clear crystals. The same crystal can be found as a large, single point or a cluster, big or small. Is the stone polished or not? Polished stones feel smooth. Many have been tumbled to soften rough edges. Tumbling stones can dramatically affect their appearance, especially if they are opaque. Colors in which each crystal is found are listed, together with countries of origin, so that you can identify unknown stones.

RIGHT Shaping, smoothing, and polishing affect the look of a crystal. Here, an Amethyst point (top) has been shaped to a palm stone (bottom).

CRYSTALS FOR SPECIFIC AILMENTS AND CONDITIONS

TOURMALINE

IN CASE OF SERIOUS ILLNESS, ALWAYS CONSULT YOUR MEDICAL PRACTITIONER

A

ACNE
Amethyst (elixir)

ADDICTIONS
Amethyst, Kunzite

ALTITUDE SICKNESS
Cuprite

ALZHEIMER'S
Chalcedony,
Blue Obsidian

ANEMIA
Bloodstone, Citrine,
Kunzite, Tourmaline,
Ruby, Tiger's Eye

ANGINA
Dioptase, Emerald

ANOREXIA
Rose Quartz

APPENDICITIS
Chrysolite

ARTHRITIS
Amethyst (elixir), Azurite, Blue Lace Agate, Black
Tourmaline, Carnelian, Chrysocolla, Fluorite,
Malachite, Rhodonite, Garnet

ASSIMILATE CALCIUM AND MAGNESIUM
Serpentine, Yellow Kunzite

ASSIMILATE IRON
Rhodonite

CITRINE

DANBURITE

ASSIMILATE MINERALS
Chalcedony, Blue Jasper

ASSIMILATE PROTEINS
Opal

ASSIMILATE VITAMINS AND MINERALS
Garnet

ASSIMILATE VITAMINS A AND E
Blue-Green Obsidian

ASTHMA
Amber, Amethyst, Malachite, Magnetite, Rose Quartz,
Dark Blue Sapphire, Morganite, Azurite, Tiger's Eye

B

BACKACHE
Hematite, Magnetite, Malachite, Sapphire

BALANCE ORGAN FUNCTION
Magnetite

BILE DUCT
Jasper

BIRTH CONTRACTIONS, STRENGTHEN
Peridot

BLACKOUTS
Lapis Lazuli

AMETHYST

BLADDER
Amber, Jasper, Orange Calcite

BLEEDING, STOP
Bloodstone, Ruby, Sapphire

BLOATING, DISPERSE
Green Jasper

BLOOD, CIRCULATION
Fire Agate

BLOOD, CLEANSING
Amethyst, Aquamarine, Bloodstone,
Garnet, Lapis Lazuli

BLOOD CLOTS
Amethyst, Bloodstone, Hematite

BLOOD, OXYGENIZE
Amethyst, Carnelian

CHRYSOPRASE

C

CANDIDA ALBICANS
Carnelian

CATARRH
Topaz

CHEMOTHERAPY
Smoky Quartz,
Herkimer Diamond

CHICKENPOX
Azurite, Malachite, Topaz

CHILDBIRTH, TO AID
Moonstone, Amber, Lapis Lazuli

CHROMOSOME DAMAGE
Chiastolite

COLDS/FEVERS
Jet, Emerald

COLIC
Carnelian

COMPUTER STRESS
Fluorite

CONCUSSION
Beryl

CONSTIPATION
Amber, Ruby

COUGH
Amber, Topaz

CRAMP
Bloodstone

 TOPAZ

SUGILITE

D

DEBILITATING ILLNESS
Black Tourmaline

DETOXIFICATION
Charoite, Jade, Peridot

DIABETES
Citrine, Jade, Serpentine

DIARRHEA
Quartz (clear), Malachite

DYSLEXIA
Sugilite

BLOOD POISONING
Carnelian

BLOOD PRESSURE, BALANCE
Aventurine, Charoite, Tourmaline

BLOOD PRESSURE, HIGH
Chrysoprase, Jadeite

BLOOD PRESSURE, LOW
Sodalite, Tourmaline

BONE MARROW
Violet Fluorite, Onyx

BONES, STRENGTHEN
Calcite, Onyx, Fluorite, Selenite,
Sardonyx, Iron Pyrite,
Amazonite

BOWELS
Jasper

BRAIN, IMPROVE FUNCTION
Lapis Lazuli

BRAIN FLUID, BALANCE
Blue Lace Agate

BREATHLESSNESS
Amber, Amethyst, Magnetite, Morganite

BRONCHITIS
Rutilated Quartz, Pyrolusite

BURNS
Quartz (clear), Rose Quartz
(place in cold water)

BURSITIS
Amber, Blue Lace Agate

BLUE LACE
AGATE

SMOKY
QUARTZ

91

YELLOW JASPER

E

EARACHE
Amazonite, Amber, Celestite, Tourmaline

ECZEMA
Sapphire

EMPHYSEMA
Amber, Amethyst, Dioptase, Malachite, Rhodonite,
Rose Quartz, Tiger's Eye, Morganite

ENDOCRINE BALANCE
Amber, Amethyst, Tourmaline, Jasper, Citrine, Fire
Agate, Green Quartz

ENVIRONMENTAL POLLUTION
Brown Jasper

EPILEPSY
Jasper, Lapis Lazuli, Sugilite, Tourmaline

EXHAUSTION
Yellow Jasper

EXTERNAL GROWTHS
Blue Lace Agate

EYES, INFLAMED
Blue Lace Agate (elixir), Sapphire, Chrysoprase

EYES, WATERING
Aquamarine

EYESIGHT, IMPROVE
Aquamarine, Charoite, Jade, Malachite,
Rhodochrosite, Rose Quartz, Variscite

F

FALLOPIAN TUBES
Chrysoprase

FEET, BURNING
Blue Lace Agate, Onyx

FERTILITY, IMPROVE
Carnelian, Chrysoprase, Garnet, Jade, Malachite, Rose
Quartz, Smoky Quartz

FEVERS
Red-Black Obsidian, Chiastolite, Ruby

FUNGAL INFECTIONS
Moss Agate (elixir)

G

GALL BLADDER
Carnelian, Citrine, Jasper, Topaz

GINGIVITIS
Blue Lace Agate (elixir as mouthwash)

GLANDS, SWOLLEN
Aquamarine, Blue Lace Agate, Topaz

GLANDULAR FEVER
Blue Lace Agate

GOITER
Amber

GOUT
Chrysoprase, Topaz, Tourmaline

GUMS
Pyrolusite, Agate

H

HAYFEVER
Blue Lace Agate

HEADACHE
Amber, Amethyst, Emerald, Lapis Lazuli, Turquoise,
Sugilite (with Black Manganese), Charoite, Cat's Eye,
Hematite, Citrine, Moonstone

HEARING LOSS
Rhodonite, Tourmaline

HEART ATTACK
Dioptase

HEARTBURN
Dioptase, Quartz (clear),
Peridot

CAT'S EYE

PERIDOT

HEAT STROKE
Blue Lace Agate

HERPES
Jadeite, Lapis Lazuli

HIP PAIN
Azurite

HIV AND AIDS
Jadeite, Lapis Lazuli, Amethyst

HORMONE PRODUCTION
Amethyst

HYDROCEPHALUS
Blue Lace Agate (elixir)

HYPERTENSION
Chrysocolla

NEPHRITE

JADEITE

J

JAUNDICE
Jadeite

JOINT PROBLEMS
Azurite

K

KIDNEY DISEASE
Jadeite, Nephrite

KNEE PROBLEMS
Azurite, Green Jadeite

L

LACTATION
Chalcedony, Chiastolite

LARYNGITIS
Amber, Blue Lace Agate, Tourmaline, Sodalite

LEG CRAMPS
Hematite

LEUKEMIA
Chrysocolla

LIVER FUNCTION
Amethyst, Aquamarine, Beryl, Bloodstone, Charoite,
Jasper, Jade, Topaz

LOWER BACK PROBLEMS
Carnelian

LUMBAGO
Magnetite

LUNGS, FUNCTION
Rhodochrosite, Chrysocolla

LUNGS, POLLUTION
Turquoise

LYMPHATIC FUNCTION
Tourmaline

LABRADORITE

I

IMMUNE SYSTEM, STRENGTHEN
Amethyst, Lapis Lazuli, Malachite, Jade, Quartz
(clear), Tourmaline, Smithsonite

IMPOTENCE
Amazonite, Variscite

INFERTILITY
Rose Quartz, Carnelian, Chrysoprase, Smoky Quartz,
Jade

INSOMNIA
Amethyst, Lepidolite, Sapphire, Sodalite, Topaz,
Chrysoprase, Lapis Lazuli, Citrine, Tourmaline, Iron
Pyrite, Labradorite

INSULIN REGULATION
Chrysocolla, Opal

**INTERNAL INFECTIONS (EAR, SINUS,
ETC.)**
Rhodochrosite (elixir, poultice), Opal

ITCHING
Azurite, Malachite

RUBY

M

M.E.
Ruby, Tourmaline

MEASLES
Turquoise

MÉNIÈRE'S DISEASE
Dioptase

MENOPAUSAL SYMPTOMS
Lapis Lazuli, Garnet, Ruby, Lepidolite

MENSTRUAL PAIN
Rose Quartz, Lapis Lazuli

MENSTRUAL PROBLEMS
Jet, Moonstone, Unakite

METABOLIC IMBALANCES
Amethyst, Cuprite, Chrysocolla, Sodalite, Moonstone,
Labradorite, Pyrolusite

MIGRAINE
Lapis Lazuli

MUMPS
Aquamarine, Topaz

MUSCLE CRAMPS
Chrysocolla, Dioptase, Hematite

MUSCLE STRAIN
Magnetite

MOONSTONE

N

NAUSEA
Jasper, Emerald

NEPHRITIS
Nephrite, Jadeite

NEURALGIA
Lapis Lazuli, Carnelian, Amber, Amethyst

NOSE BLEED
Carnelian

O

OBESITY
Green Tourmaline

OSTEOPOROSIS
Amazonite

SODALITE

CARNELIAN

P

PAIN RELIEF
Lapis Lazuli, Magnetite, Dioptase, Rose Quartz,
Turquoise, Carnelian, Malachite, Carnelian

PARKINSON'S DISEASE
Opal

PITUITARY GLAND IMBALANCE
Benitoite

PNEUMONIA
Fluorite

PROSTATE GLAND
Chrysoprase

PSORIASIS
Blue Lace Agate, Labradorite

R

RADIATION-RELATED ILLNESS/THERAPY
Smoky Quartz, Herkimer Diamond,
Yellow Kunzite, Malachite, Sodalite

RHEUMATISM
Agate, Amber, Azurite, Carnelian, Chrysocolla,
Fluorite, Malachite

 S

SCAR TISSUE
Rose Quartz

SCIATICA
Tourmaline, Sapphire

SEXUALLY TRANSMITTED DISEASES
Chrysoprase

SEXUAL LIBIDO, TO REKINDLE
Fluorite

SINUS
Azurite, Blue Lace Agate

SKIN PROBLEMS
Aquamarine (elixir)

SORE THROAT
Amber, Aquamarine, Beryl, Lapis Lazuli, Blue
Tourmaline

SORES
Chalcedony

SPINAL ALIGNMENT
Azurite, Hematite, Labradorite, Magnetite,
Tourmaline, White Jade

SPORTS INJURIES
Magnetite

T

THYMUS, STIMULATE
Aventurine, Dioptase, Quartz (clear)

THYROID, BALANCE
Rhodochrosite (elixir), Citrine

THYROID, SEDATE
Turquoise, Sodalite

TISSUE REGENERATION
Peridot

TOOTH DECAY
Amazonite, Fluorite, Onyx

TOOTHACHE
Amber, Aquamarine, Lapis Lazuli

TRAVEL SICKNESS
Jasper

TUBERCULOSIS
Morganite

TUMORS
Amethyst, Bloodstone,
Smoky Quartz

 U

ULCERS
Chrysocolla

 V

VARICOSE VEINS
Blue Lace Agate, Bloodstone,
Amber

VERTIGO
Quartz (clear), Cuprite

VIRILITY, IMPROVE
Lapis Lazuli, Jet, Black Quartz,
Red-Black Obsidian

VOMITING
Lapis Lazuli

W

WATER RETENTION
Cuprite

WHOOPING COUGH
Topaz, Amber, Blue Lace Agate

LAPIS LUZULI

DIOPTASE

AZURITE

95

CRYSTALS AND THE BODY

The Chakras

When healing and balancing the chakras, an appropriate stone is placed on the chakra –
on the front or back of the body, whichever is most comfortable. Stones can be placed
on all the chakras, or above the head and below the feet to perform certain tasks.

HIGHER CROWN

CROWN

BROW/ THIRD EYE

THROAT

HIGHER
HEART

HEART

SOLAR
PLEXUS

SACRAL

BASE

EARTH

GROUNDING ENERGY FROM CROWN TO BASE: Smoky Quartz

OPENING AND CLEANSING ALL: *Amber, Dendritic Agate, Malachite*

CLEANSING AND PROTECTING ALL: *Tourmaline, Garnet*

ALIGNING: *Boji Stone, Yellow Kunzite, Kyanite*

ELEVATING: *Turquoise*

CLEANSE LOWER CHAKRAS: *Bloodstone*

HIGHER CROWN	*Kunzite, Apophyllite, Celestite, Muscovite, Selenite, Petalite, Azeztulite, Phenacite*
CROWN	*Moldavite, Citrine, Quartz, Red Serpentine, Purple Jasper, Clear Tourmaline, Golden Beryl, Lepidolite, Purple Sapphire*
BROW/THIRD EYE	*Apophyllite, Sodalite, Moldavite, Azurite, Herkimer Diamond, Lapis Lazuli, Garnet, Purple Fluorite, Kunzite, Lepidolite, Malachite with Azurite, Royal Sapphire, Electric Blue Obsidian, Azeztulite, Antacamite*
THROAT	*Azurite, Turquoise, Amethyst, Aquamarine, Blue Topaz, Blue Tourmaline, Amber, Kunzite, Amethyst, Lepidolite, Blue Obsidian, Petalite*
HIGHER HEART	*Dioptase, Kunzite*
HEART	*Rose Quartz, Green Quartz, Aventurine, Kunzite, Variscite, Muscovite, Red Calcite, Rhodonite, Watermelon Tourmaline, Pink Tourmaline, Green Tourmaline, Peridot, Apophyllite, Lepidolite, Morganite, Green Quartz, Pink Danburite, Ruby, Chrysocolla, Green Sapphire*
SOLAR PLEXUS	*Malachite, Jasper, Tiger's Eye, Citrine, Yellow Tourmaline, Golden Beryl, Rhodochrosite, Smithsonite*
SACRAL	*Blue Jasper, Red Jasper, Orange Carnelian, Topaz, Orange Calcite, Citrine*
BASE	*Azurite, Bloodstone, Chrysocolla, Obsidian, Golden Yellow Topaz, Black Tourmaline, Carnelian, Citrine, Red Jasper, Smoky Quartz*
EARTH	*Boji Stone, Fire Agate, Brown Jasper, Smoky Quartz, Hematite, Mahogany, Obsidian, Tourmaline, Rhodonite, Cuprite*

CRYSTAL AFFINITIES

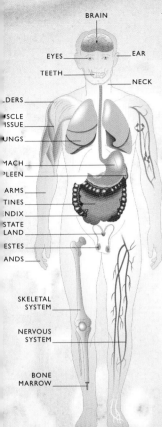

BRAIN
EYES — EAR
TEETH
NECK
...LDERS
...SCLE ...ISSUE
...UNGS
...MACH
...LEEN
ARMS
...TINES
...NDIX
...STATE
...LAND
...ESTES
...ANDS
SKELETAL SYSTEM
NERVOUS SYSTEM
BONE MARROW

BRAIN *Amber, Green Tourmaline, Dark Blue Tourmaline, Beryl, Blue Lace Agate*

EAR *Amber, Red-Black and Snowflake Obsidian, Celestite, Rhodonite, Orange Calcite*

EYES *Aquamarine, Beryl, Chalcedony, Chrysoprase, Sapphire, Charoite, Dark Blue Tourmaline, Celestite, Blue Fluorite, Fire Agate, Cat's Eye, Orange Calcite*

TEETH *Aquamarine, Rutilated Quartz, Fluorite*

NECK *Aquamarine, Quartz*

SHOULDER *Selenite*

MUSCLE TISSUE *Cuprite, Magnetite, Danburite*

LUNGS *Beryl, Pink Tourmaline, Peridot, Rhodonite, Amber, Dioptase, Kunzite, Lapis Lazuli, Turquoise, Rhodochrosite, Sardonyx, Blue Tourmaline, Chrysocolla, Emerald, Morganite*

SPLEEN *Amber, Aquamarine, Azurite, Bloodstone, Chalcedony, Red Obsidian*

STOMACH *Green Fluorite, Fire Agate, Beryl*

INTESTINES *Beryl, Peridot, Celestite, Green Fluorite*

APPENDIX *Chrysolite*

ARMS *Malachite, Jadeite*

PROSTATE GLAND *Chrysoprase*

TESTES *Jadeite, Topaz, Carnelian, Variscite*

HANDS *Moldavite, Aquamarine, Moonstone*

SKELETAL SYSTEM *Amazonite, Azurite, Chrysocolla, Calcite, Cuprite, Fluorite, Dendritic Agate, Purple Fluorite, Sardonyx, Iron Pyrite*

NERVOUS SYSTEM/ NEUROLOGICAL TISSUE *Amber, Green Jade, Lapis Lazuli, Green Tourmaline, Dendritic Agate*

BONE MARROW *Purple Fluorite*

PINEAL GLAND *Gem Rhodonite*

PITUITARY GLAND *Benitoite*

JAW *Aquamarine*

THROAT *Aquamarine, Beryl, Lapis Lazuli, Blue Tourmaline, Amber, Green Jasper*

THYROID *Amber, Aquamarine, Azurite, Blue Tourmaline, Citrine*

THYMUS *Aventurine, Blue Tourmaline*

HEART *Cuprite, Rose Quartz, Charoite, Rhodonite, Garnet, Dioptase*

LIVER *Aquamarine, Beryl, Bloodstone, Carnelian, Red Jasper, Charoite, Danburite*

GALL BLADDER *Carnelian, Jasper, Topaz, Calcite, Citrine, Yellow Quartz, Tiger's Eye, Chalcedony, Danburite*

KIDNEYS *Aquamarine, Beryl, Bloodstone, Hematite, Jadeite, Nephrite, Rose Quartz, Citrine, Orange Calcite, Smoky Quartz, Amber, Muscovite*

PANCREAS *Red Tourmaline, Blue Lace Agate, Chrysocolla*

SPINE *Garnet, Tourmaline, Labradorite, Beryl*

FALLOPIAN TUBES *Chrysoprase*

FEMALE REPRODUCTIVE SYSTEM *Carnelian, Moonstone, Chrysoprase, Amber, Topaz, Unakite*

BLADDER *Topaz, Jasper, Amber, Orange Calcite*

CIRCULATORY SYSTEM AND BLOOD *Amethyst, Bloodstone, Chalcedony, Cuprite, Hematite, Red Jasper*

VEINS *Variscite, Pyrolusite, Snowflake Obsidian*

KNEES *Azurite, Jadeite*

JOINTS *Calcite, Azurite, Rhodonite, Magnetite*

SKIN *Azurite, Brown Jasper, Green Jasper*

FEET *Onyx, Smoky Quartz, Apophyllite*

ENDOCRINE SYSTEM *Amber, Amethyst, Yellow Jasper, Pink Tourmaline, Fire Agate*

IMMUNE SYSTEM *Amethyst, Black Tourmaline, Lapis Lazuli, Malachite, Turquoise*

DIGESTIVE TRACT *Chrysocolla, Red Jade, Green Jasper*

METABOLISM *Amethyst, Sodalite, Pyrolusite*

BACK *Malachite, Sapphire, Lapis Lazuli*

LOWER BACK *Carnelian*

CAPILLARIES *Dendritic Agate*

PINEAL GLAND
PITUITARY GLAND
JAW
THROAT
THYROID
THYMUS
HEART
LIVER
GALL BLADDER
KIDNEYS
PANCREAS
SPINE
FALLOPIAN TUBES
REPRODUCTIVE SYSTEM
BLADDER
CIRCULATORY SYSTEM
VEINS
KNEES
JOINTS
SKIN
FEET

CRYSTALS FOR THE AURA

AMBER
An ancient protector. It aligns the aura with the physical body, mind, and spirit. It draws off negative energy and so cleans the aura.

AMBER

AMETHYST

AMETHYST
Gently cleanses the aura, heals holes, and protects it, drawing in divine energy.

APACHE TEAR (CLEAR BLACK OBSIDIAN)
Gently protects the aura from absorbing negative energies.

APACHE TEAR

BLOODSTONE

BLACK JADE
Guards the aura against negativity.

BLOODSTONE
Etheric cleanser that greatly benefits the aura.

CITRINE
Cleanses and aligns the aura, filling in gaps.

CITRINE

TOURMALINE

FLUORITE AND TOURMALINE
Provide a psychic shield.

GREEN TOURMALINE
Heals holes in the aura.

JET
Protects the aura against other people's negative thoughts.

LABRADORITE

KUNZITE

LABRADORITE
Prevents energy leakage. It protects by aligning to spiritual energy.

MAGNETITE
Strengthens the aura.

QUARTZ
Cleanses, protects, and increases the auric field, sealing any holes.

GREEN TOURMALINE

QUARTZ

KUNZITE AND SELENITE
Detach mental influences from the aura.

PETALITE
Highest vibration. Releases negative karma and entities from the aura.

MAGNETITE

JET

SMOKY QUARTZ
Grounds energy and dissolves negative patterns encased in the aura.

PETALITE

SMOKY QUARTZ

SELENITE

GEM REMEDIES

CHRYSOCOLLA

BLACK TOURMALINE	Provides psychic protection and screens from electro-magnetic stress. Relieves jet lag. Releases toxic energy from emotions, mind, and body.
MALACHITE	Harmonizes physical, mental, emotional, and spiritual; grounds the body. Use tumbled stone only.
FLUORITE	Breaks up blockages in the etheric body. Anti-viral.
JADEITE	Heals eye conditions, brings peace.
AMAZONITE	Balances the metabolism.
GREEN JASPER	Restores biorhythms and natural sexuality.
HEMATITE	Strengthens boundaries.
KUNZITE	Opens the heart.
AMBER	Acts as an antibiotic, heals throat problems.
GOLDEN BERYL	A gargle for sore throats.
BLOODSTONE	Releases constipation and emotional stagnation.
CHAROITE	An excellent cleanser for the body.
HERKIMER DIAMOND	Aids psychic vision and dream recall.
MOSS AGATE	Treats fungal infections.

MOLDAVITE	Aids staying in the present moment, releasing from past.
AQUAMARINE/ AVENTURINE	Aid in the case of skin problems.
AQUAMARINE	Calms mental stress and overactive mind.
AVENTURINE	Increases stamina to see things through, integrates new experiences.
RHODOCHROSITE	Treats infections, promotes thyroid balance, heals the heart.
TIGER'S EYE	Aids self-empowerment.
SAPPHIRE	Removes toxins from the body.
BLUE LACE AGATE	Balances brain fluid, mouthwash for gingivitis, bath for inflamed eyes.
AMAZONITE	Balances metabolism.
AMETHYST	Treats acne and arthritis.
QUARTZ	An energy enhancer and general cleanser.
CARNELIAN	Reenergizes.
CITRINE	Clears mental confusion, improves concentration and decision-making processes.
CHRYSOCOLLA	Releases unresolved grief.

If in doubt, consult a qualified crystal therapist.

MOSS AGATE

GOLDEN BERYL

GEMSTONES

DIAMOND (UNCUT)

RUBY (UNPOLISHED)

RUBY RINGS

DIAMOND

SOURCE: South Africa, Australia, Brazil, India, Russia, United States.

APPEARANCE: Bright, transparent when polished. *Colors:* Clear, yellow, blue.

PROPERTIES: Bonds relationships, brings love and clarity; amplifies energy. Qualities include fearlessness, invincibility, fortitude, purity. Aids glaucoma.

POSITION: Finger, temple.

RUBY

SOURCE: India, Madagascar, Russia, Sri Lanka, Cambodia, Kenya.

APPEARANCE: Bright, transparent when polished, opaque when not. *Color:* Red.

PROPERTIES: Energizes, balances, may overstimulate, brings up anger or negative energy for transmutation. Leadership. Stimulates heart chakra: "following your bliss." Shields against psychic attack, promotes positive dreams. Aids in retaining wealth, passion. Detoxifies body, blood; treats fevers, restricted blood flow.

POSITION: Heart, finger, ankle.

SAPPHIRE

SOURCE: Burma, Czech Republic, Slovakia, Brazil, Kenya, India.

APPEARANCE: Bright, transparent when polished. *Colors:* Blue, yellow, green, black, purple.

PROPERTIES: Relaxes, focuses, calms mind, releases unwanted thoughts, mental tension. Peace of mind, serenity. Aligns physical, mental, spiritual planes, restores balance within body. Releases depression, spiritual confusion, aids concentration. Heals eye, removes impurities and stress. Brings prosperity, attracts gifts, releases frustration. Treats disorders of blood, alleviates excessive bleeding. Strengthens veins, improves elasticity. **Yellow Sapphire:** Attracts wealth to home. Stimulates intellect, overall focus. Elixir removes toxins from body. **Purple Sapphire:** Awakens. Useful for meditation, kundalini rise; stimulates crown chakra, opens spirituality. **Black Sapphire:** Protects, centers. Imparts confidence in own intuition. Promotes employment prospects and retaining job. **Green Sapphire:** Improves vision, aids dream remembrance. Stimulates heart chakra, brings loyalty, fidelity. **Royal Sapphire:** Eliminates negative energies from chakras, stimulates third eye to access information for growth. Teaches self-responsibility for thoughts and feelings. Treats brain disorders, including dyslexia.

POSITION: Touching body. Finger.

BLUE SAPPHIRE

SAPPHIRE (UNCUT)

YELLOW SAPPHIRE

BLACK SAPP

EMERALD
(UNCUT)

AQUAMARINE
(UNPOLISHED)

EMERALD JEWELRY

EMERALD

SOURCE: India, Zimbabwe, Tanzania, Brazil, Egypt, Austria.

APPEARANCE: Bright, transparent when polished. *Color:* Green.

PROPERTIES: Gives physical, emotional, mental equilibrium; focuses intention, raises consciousness, fosters positive action. Provides inspiration, infinite patience; enhances psychic abilities, wisdom from mental plane. Strengthens memory, aids eloquence, promotes truth, inspires deep inner knowing. "Successful love," domestic bliss, and loyalty. Treats lungs, heart, spine, muscles; soothes eyes.

POSITION: Little finger, ring finger, over heart, on right arm. Do not wear constantly.

AQUAMARINE

SOURCE: United States, Mexico, Russia, Brazil, India, Ireland, Zimbabwe, Afghanistan.

APPEARANCE: Clear crystal. *Color:* Pale Purple, blue tinge.

PROPERTIES: Reduces stress, quietens mind, sharpens intellect, clears blocked communication chakra. Filters information reaching brain, aids interpretation of emotional state. Reduces fear, increases sensitivity, creativity; enhances intuition, spiritual awareness. Shields aura, aligns chakras. Brings tolerance and responsibility. Treats swollen glands, sore throats; strengthens organs, liver, spleen, kidneys; aids teeth, jaw, eyes, throat, stomach.

POSITION: Place as appropriate.

GARNET
(TUMBLED)

PERIDOT
(UNCUT)

TOPAZ

GARNET

SOURCE: Worldwide.

APPEARANCE: Transparent or translucent crystal. *Colors:* Red, green (Almandine).

PROPERTIES: Energizes, revitalizes; balances energy, brings serenity. Activates other crystals, clears negative chakra energy. Inspires love, stimulates controlled rise of kundalini energy. Past-life recall: place on the third eye. Treats spinal and cellular disorders, blood, hearts, lungs; regenerates DNA. Aids assimilation of minerals/vitamins. **Red Garnet:** Represents love. Attuned to heart energy, revitalizes feelings, enhances sexuality. Controls anger, especially toward oneself.

POSITION: Earlobes, finger, or over heart.

PERIDOT (Olivine/Chrysolite)

SOURCE: United States, Brazil, Egypt, Ireland, Russia.

APPEARANCE: Clear crystal when polished. *Color:* Olive green.

PROPERTIES: Cleanses subtle, physical bodies, mind. Releases negative patterns, vibrations; promotes clarity, well-being. Releases, neutralizes toxins on all levels. Visionary, understands destiny, purpose, helpful to healers. Opens, cleanses heart and solar plexus chakras, regulates cycles of life. Alleviates jealousy, anger; reduces stress; motivates growth, necessary change. Tonic effect, heals, strengthens. Heart, lungs, spleen, intestinal tract, ulcers; strengthens eyes. Aids birth contractions.

POSITION: Throat and as appropriate.

PERIDOT

TOPAZ

SOURCE: United States, Mexico, India, Australia, South Africa.

APPEARANCE: Transparent, pointed crystals, sometimes large.

Colors: Golden yellow, brown, blue.

PROPERTIES: Directs energy. Soothes, heals, stimulates, recharges, remotivates. Promotes truth, forgiveness. Sheds light on path, taps into inner resources. Brings joy, generosity, good health. Cleans aura.

Golden Topaz: Recharges and strengthens faith and optimism. Attracts helpful people.

Blue Topaz: Aids throat chakra and verbalization (place on throat chakra).

POSITION: Ring finger or place as appropriate.

GREEN GARNET
(ALMANDINE ON MATRIX)

GARNET RING

OPAL

COMMON OPAL

RED SPINEL
(ON MATRIX)

POLISHED OPAL

OPAL

SOURCE: Australia, Mexico, Peru.

APPEARANCE: Iridescent, fiery. *Colors:* White, black shot with many colors.

PROPERTIES: Enhances cosmic consciousness, originality, dynamic creativity. Fosters love, passion. Induces visions. Brings loyalty, faithfulness, spontaneity. Amplifies traits. Emotionally stability. Treats Parkinson's disease, infections, fevers, strengthens memory, purifies blood and kidneys, regulates insulin, eases childbirth. **Fire Opal:** Symbol of hope, excellent for business.

POSITION: Wear on little finger.

SPINEL

SOURCE: Canada, Sri Lanka, Burma, India.

APPEARANCE: Crystalline with terminations, or tumbled pebbles. *Colors:* Colorless, white, red, blue, violet, black, green, yellow, orange, brown.

PROPERTIES: Energy renewal, encouragement, and rejuvenation. Accepts success with humility. Facilitates movement of kundalini energy. **Brown Spinel:** Cleanses the aura and opens links to physical body. Opens the earth chakra and grounds. **Red Spinel:** Stimulates physical vitality and strength. Arouses kundalini. Opens and aligns base chakra. **Orange Spinel:** Stimulates creativity and intuition, balances emotions, treats infertility. Opens and aligns navel chakra. **Yellow Spinel:** Stimulates intellect and personal power. Opens and aligns solar plexus chakra. **Green Spinel:** Stimulates love, compassion and kindness. Opens and aligns heart chakra. **Blue Spinel:** Stimulates communication and channeling. Calms sexual desire. Opens and aligns throat chakra. **Dark Blue Spinel:** Stimulates psychic abilities, aligns with higher self, facilitates astral travel. Opens and aligns brow (third eye) chakra. **Violet Spinel:** Stimulates spiritual development and astral travel. Opens and aligns crown chakra. **Colorless Spinel:** Stimulates mysticism and higher communication. Links chakras on physical body with crown chakra of etheric body, facilitating visions and enlightenment. **Black Spinel:** Stimulates insights as to material problems, for example, financial worries or moving home. Protective; earths energy to balance rise of kundalini.

POSITION: Lay on chakras, or wear as appropriate.

CLEAR CRYSTALS

QUARTZ

PHANTOM QUARTZ

RUTILATED QUARTZ
(TUMBLED)

BLUE QUARTZ

TOURMALINATED
QUARTZ

QUARTZ

SOURCE: Throughout the world.

APPEARANCE: Long, pointed crystals, transparent, milky or striated. *Colors:* Clear, smoky, blue, green, yellow.

PROPERTIES: Most powerful healer. Energy amplifier, stores, releases, regulates energy. Generates electromagnetism, dispels static electricity. Cleans, enhances subtle bodies. Deep soul cleanser. Dissolves karmic seeds. Enhances psychic abilities. Connects physical dimension with mind. Stimulates immune system. Soothes burns. Reduces fuel consumption. **Blue Quartz:** Assists in reaching out to others, assuages fear. **Green Quartz:** Opens, stabilizes heart chakra. Transmutes negative energy, inspires creativity, balances endocrine system. **Golden Healer (Coated Yellow-Orange):** Facilitates spiritual communication over a long distance, including between the worlds, and empowers healing.

POSITION: Place as appropriate.

PHANTOM QUARTZ

APPEARANCE: White or colored crystal encompassed within the main crystal.

PROPERTIES: Increases universal awareness, aids healing the planet and activates healing abilities, brings forth a spiritual guide, facilitates reading past lives. Treats hearing disorders and opens clairaudience. **Amethyst Phantom Quartz:** Accesses prebirth state and plan for the future.

POSITION: Wear or place as appropriate.

TOURMALINATED QUARTZ

APPEARANCE: Long, thick, dark "threads" through clear crystal.

PROPERTIES: Dissolves crystallized patterns,

CATHEDRAL QUARTZ

harmonizes disparate and opposite elements. Harmonizes polarities. Problem solver.

POSITION: Place as appropriate.

RUTILATED QUARTZ

APPEARANCE: Long thin "threads" in clear crystal.

PROPERTIES: Reaches root of problems. Aids astral travel. Absorbs mercury poisoning. Heightens energetic impulse of quartz.

POSITION: Neck for thyroid; heart for thymus; solar plexus for energy; ears to balance and align.

SMOKY QUARTZ

APPEARANCE: Translucent, long, pointed crystals darker ends. Note: Very dark quartz is usually artificially irradiated and should not be used. *Color:* Brownish to blackish hue.

PROPERTIES: Elimination and detoxification at all levels. Relieves fear, lifts depression, brings calmness, positive thought. Treats radiation related illness or chemotherapy. Aids acceptance of body, strenghtens virility, cleans base chakra. Grounds spiritual energy, neutralizes negative energy and geopathic stress. Alleviates nightmares, manifests dreams.

POSITION: Anywhere, especially base chakra. Under pillow, by telephone, or on geopathic stress lines.

ROSE QUARTZ

APPEARANCE: Usually translucent, may be transparent. *Color:* pink.

PROPERTIES: Unconditional love, heals and opens heart, calms, reassures, deep inner healing. Releases unexpressed emotions, soothes internalized pain. If never received love, opens heart. Aids positive affirmations, self-trust and self-worth. Teaches how to love one's self, encourages self-forgiveness and acceptance. Aids physical heart and circulatory system. Said to increase fertility. Soothes burns, blistering.

POSITION: Over heart or by bed.

ROSE QUARTZ

AMETHYST

SOURCE: United States, Canada, Brazil, Mexico, Russia, Sri Lanka, Uruguay, East Africa.

APPEARANCE: Transparent, pointed quartz crystal. *Colors:* Pale to dark purple.

PROPERTIES: Powerful healer, protector, enhances psychic abilities, spiritual awareness. Stimulates throat chakra, clears aura, transmutes negative energy. Calms mind, enhances meditation, visualization. Disperses psychic attack. Ameliorates anger, rage, fear, resentment. Aids assimilation of ideas. Connects cause and effect. Promotes selflessness. Effects enhanced by Rose Quartz. Supports sobriety. Relieves physical, emotional pain. Boosts hormones. Strengthens, cleanses organs and circulatory system, calms nervous system, unites scattered energies. Aids insomnia, hearing, endocrine glands, digestive tract, heart, cellular disorder.

Violet Amethyst: Lighter vibration that works on profoundly spiritual level.

POSITION: All parts of the body, especially throat and chest, or as appropriate.

SMOKY QUARTZ

AMETHYST GEODE
(WITH SHOW QUARTZ CRYSTAL)

105

AMTRINE

AZEZTULITE

DIOPTASE

AMETRINE

SOURCE: Bolivia.

APPEARANCE: Combination of Amethyst and Citrine. *Colors:* Purple and yellow.

PROPERTIES: Powerfully combines properties of two crystals, fast and effective. Enhances well-being, brings universal equilibrium, connects physical with higher consciousness, facilitates astral travel and mental clarity. Aids thinking things through. Releases blockages on all levels including negative emotional programing and prejudice. Relieves psychic attack. Balances male–female. Disperses negativity from aura and toxins from body, energizes with light. Enhances compatibility and acceptance of others. Aids autonomic nervous system and physical maturation, stablizes DNA/RNA, oxygenates body, cleanses blood. Heals M.E., burning sensations, depression, gastric disturbances, fatigue and lethargy.

POSITION: Wear for prolonged periods, place on solar plexus.

CITRINE: See page 109.

AQUA AURA

SOURCE: Synthetic color on Quartz

APPEARANCE: Clear or cloudy quartz crystals artificially bonded with gold. *Colors:* Blue, red, purple.

PROPERTIES: Intense energy, frees from limitations. Creates space for something new. Heals, cleanses, and calms the aura, releases stress, activates chakras, releases negativity from subtle bodies, stimulates channeling and self-expression, deepens spiritual attunement and communication. Safeguards against psychic or psychological attack. Enhances healing properties of other crystals. Aids thymus gland and immune system.

POSITION: Hold, wear, or place as appropriate.

AQUA AURA

AZEZTULITE

SOURCE: Extremely rare: one seam, mined out.

APPEARANCE: Clear quartz with striations. *Color:* Colorless.

PROPERTIES: High vibration, attuned to high frequencies. Strongly positive, never requires cleansing. Facilitates meditation, providing protective spiral. Opens third eye and higher crown chakras. Activates ascension points. Used on third eye, aids seeing future. Treats cancer, cellular disorders, inflammation.

POSITION: Third eye, crown, or as appropriate.

DIOPTASE

SOURCE: Iran, Russia, Namibia, Zaire, Chile, Peru.

APPEARANCE: Small transparent crystals. *Colors:* Very deep green-blue, green.

PROPERTIES: Brings all chakras to higher level of functioning, opens higher heart chakra, induces spiritual attunement. Promotes living in present moment, activates past-life memory. Powerful

**BLUE KYANITE
(ON QUARTZ MATRIX)**

disorders, fevers, urogenital system, thyroid and parathyroid, adrenal glands, throat, brain.

Blue Kyanite: Strengthens the voice.

POSITION: As appropriate, particularly between navel and heart. Wear as pendant.

PETALITE

SOURCE: Brazil, Madagascar.

APPEARANCE: Quartzlike, striated, slightly iridescent. *Colors:* Clear, white, pink, gray, reddish-white, greenish-white.

PROPERTIES: High vibration, opens to cosmic consciousness. Protective, enhances meditation, attunement, communication, and angelic connections, moves beyond psychic abilities, provides safe environment for spiritual contact or vision quest. Activates and energizes. Grounds during spiritual activity. Shamanic crystal. Calms aura. Opens throat and higher crown chakras. Releases negative karma and entities. Aids tie cutting. Harmonizes endocrine system. Treats AIDS, cancer, cells, eyes, lungs, muscles, and intestines.

Pink Petalite: Clears heart meridian, strengthens emotional body, releases fear and worry.

Clear Petalite: Renders negative energies impotent.

POSITION: Wear or place as appropriate.

PETALITE

PHENACITE

SOURCE: Madagascar, Russia, Zimbabwe, Colorado, Brazil.

APPEARANCE: Glassy, quartz-like. *Colors:* Colorless, yellow, yellow-red, red, pink, brown.

PROPERTIES: Highest vibration, interdimensional, purifying, and integrating. Activates healing from etheric body to physical. Cleanses and activates the chakras.

Clear Phenacite: Interdimensional travel.

Yellow Phenacite: Extra-terrestrial contact.

POSITION: Wear as faceted stone or place as appropriate, especially above head.

PHENACITE

physical and mental healer, regulates cell disorder, activates T-cells, relieves Ménière's disease, eases high blood pressure, alleviates pain including migraine. Said to prevent heart attacks and heal heart conditions.

POSITION: Higher Heart chakra.

KYANITE

SOURCE: Brazil.

APPEARANCE: Striated or layered crystal, often transparent or "pearlized." *Color:* Blue-white, pink, green, yellow, gray, black.

PROPERTIES: Excellent for attunement and meditation. Calming and tranquilizing. Aids self-expression, communication, and psychic abilities. Connects to guides. Supports continuation of difficult projects. Instills compassion. Aligns chakras and subtle bodies instantly. Dispels blockages, confusion, illusion, anger and frustration. Restores Qi. Never requires cleaning, does not hold negativity. Increases linear thought. Balances yin–yang. Treats muscular

107

MOLDAVITE

MOLDAVITE

SOURCE: Czech Republic, Slovakia.

APPEARANCE: Small, transparent crystals, "extra-terrestrial." Meteorite. *Color:* Dark green.

PROPERTIES: Communication with higher self, extraterrestrials. Crown chakra: opens to higher spiritual energies; on throat: communicates interplanetary messages.

POSITION: Place on forehead, crown, throat.

CELESTITE

SOURCE: Britain, Egypt, Mexico, Peru, Poland, Libya.

APPEARANCE: Transparent, pyramidal crystals. *Colors:* Blue, yellow,

PROPERTIES: Contacts spiritual and angelic realms, encourages spiritual development, enlightenment, pureness of heart. Aids clairvoyant communication, dream recall, astral travel. Disperses worries, attracts good fortune. Synthesizes instinct and intellect, aids analysis of complex ideas. Brings balance and alignment. Treats disorders of eyes and ears, balances mind. Eliminates toxins, brings cellular order.

POSITION: Place as appropriate.

DANBURITE

DANBURITE

SOURCE: United States, Czech Republic, Slovakia, Russia, Switzerland, Japan, Mexico.

APPEARANCE: Clear with striations. *Colors:* Pink, yellow, white, lilac.

PROPERTIES: Activates intellect and higher consciousness. Promotes ease, changes recalcitrant attitudes, brings patience, peace of mind. Treats liver, gall bladder. Detoxifies, adds weight. Aids muscular and motor function. **Pink Danburite:** Opens heart. **Lilac Danburite:** Opens higher chakras, raises awareness.

POSITION: Place as appropriate, especially over heart or above head.

PINK KUNZITE

BLUE CELESTITE

KUNZITE

SOURCE: United States, Madagascar, Brazil, Burma, Afghanistan.

APPEARANCE: Transparent or translucent, striated crystal. *Colors:* Pink, green, yellow, lilac.

PROPERTIES: Spiritual, produces loving thoughts and communication, radiates peace, connects to universal love. Dispels negativity. Induces deep, centered meditative state, enhances creativity. Aids self-expression; removes obstacles to path, emotional debris; allows free expression of feelings. Adjusts to pressure of life, heals psychiatric disorders. Activates heart chakra, aligns with throat and third eye. Shields from unwanted energies, dispels attached entities and mental influences from aura. Strengthens circulatory system and heart muscle. **Green Kunzite:** Grounds spiritual love. **Yellow Kunzite:** Aligns chakras, restructures DNA, deflects radiation and microwaves from auric field; stabilizes cellular blueprint and calcium–magnesium balance. **Lilac Kunzite:** Celestial Doorway. Symbol of infinity. Aids transition, imparts knowledge departed souls require, helps them move over into enlightenment. Breaks the barriers of time into the eternal moment.

POSITION: Hold or place as appropriate.

HIDDENITE

SOURCE: Brazil

APPEARANCE: Transparent with vertical striations (form of Kunzite). *Colors:* Yellow to emerald green.

PROPERTIES: As Kunzite. In addition: connects to other worlds, links intellect and love to birth the unknown and aid transfer of knowledge. Aids diagnosis.

POSITION: Hold or place on third eye.

HERKIMER DIAMOND

SOURCE: United States, Mexico, Spain.

APPEARANCE: Clear, oily, inner rainbows. *Color:* Clear.

PROPERTIES: Energizes, enlivens, promotes creativity. Aids attunement, stimulates psychic abilities, dream recall. Detoxificant, protects against radioactivity, aids insomnia caused by geopathic stress, corrects DNA, metabolic imbalances; eliminates stress. Promotes past life recall.

POSITION: Pendants, earrings, base of spine.

ANGELITE (Compressed Celestite)

SOURCE: Britain, Egypt, Mexico, Peru, Poland, Libya.

APPEARANCE: Opaque with veins and "wings." *Color:* Blue-white.

PROPERTIES: Aids angelic contact. Transmutes pain and disorder into wholeness and healing.

POSITION: Hold or place on appropriate point, or beside the bed.

AMBER

SOURCE: Britain, Baltic, Northern Germany, Poland, Italy, Romania, Russia, Burma, Dominica.

APPEARANCE: Translucent, resinous, insects trapped inside. *Colors:* Yellow through orange to brown. Green created artificially.

PROPERTIES: Brings wisdom, balance, patience, promotes altruism. Useful healer, draws disease from body, aids tissue revitalization. Heals nervous system, promotes self-healing. Elixir is antibiotic. Eases stress, neutralizes negative energy. Cleanses environment, body, mind, and spirit. Aids depression, memory, decision-making. Heals throat and Throat chakra, kidneys, bladder.

POSITION: Wrist and throat.

CITRINE (Cairngorn)

SOURCE: Britain, United States, Brazil, France, Madagascar, Russia.

APPEARANCE: Transparent, may be cloudy. *Colors:* Yellow through to brown.

PROPERTIES: Prosperity, attracts wealth, success. Brings happiness, generosity. Energizes, invigorates, increases motivation/physical energy, activates creativity. Dissipates negative energy, promotes inner calm. Alleviates depression and fears. Balahces yin—yang, opens Navel and Solar Plexus chakras, stimulates Crown chakra. Cleanses aura, aligns etheric body with physical. Treats digestive problems, thyroid imbalance, circulation of blood.

POSITION: Fingers, throat.

HIDDENITE

HERKIMER DIAMOND

ANGELITE

AMBER

CITRINE GEODE

SELENITE

SOURCE: United States, Russia, Austria, Greece, Poland, Germany, France, Britain.

APPEARANCE: Translucent with fine ribbing, may be fishtail. *Colors:* Pure white, orange, blue, brown.

PROPERTIES: Brings clarity of mind, accesses angelic consciousness. Reaches other lives. Creates protective grid. Detaches entities. Assists judgment, insight; shows inner workings. Aligns spinal column, promotes flexibility. **Brown Selenite:** Earths angelic energies. **Blue Selenite:** Quietens the intellect, reveals core of a problem.

POSITION: Hold, place in house.

SELENITE
(POLISHED)

GREEN BERYL

GOLDEN BERYL

PURPLE FLUORITE CLUSTER
WITH COLORLESS, CLEAR FLUORITE CRYSTALS.

FLUORITE

SOURCE: United States, Britain, Australia, Norway, China, Peru, Mexico.

APPEARANCE: Transparent, cubic crystals. *Colors:* Clear, blue, green, purple, yellow.

PROPERTIES: Protective, especially on psychic level and against computer and electromagnetic stress. Aids physical and mental coordination, counteracts mental disorder, increases concentration. Grounds, integrates spiritual energies. Promotes unbiased impartiality, heightens intuitive powers. Rekindles sexual libido. Benefits teeth, cells, and bones; repairs DNA damage. Powerful antiviral effect (elixir). Benefits arthritis, rheumatism. **Clear Fluorite:** Stimulates crown chakra, energizes aura, harmonizes intellect and spirit. **Blue Fluorite** Enhances orderly thought, clear communication, calms energy, treats eye problems. **Green Fluorite** Grounds excess energy, dissipates emotional trauma, clears infections. Aids stomach disorders, intestines. **Violet and Purple Fluorite:** Stimulates third eye, imparts common sense to psychic communication. Assists bones and bone marrow

disorders. **Yellow Fluorite:** Enhances creativity, stablizes group energy, releases toxins.

POSITION: Earlobes. Place on computer, etc. or as appropriate.

BERYL

SOURCE: United States, Russia, Australia, Brazil, Czech Republic, Slovakia, France, Norway.

APPEARANCE: Prismatic crystals, may be pyramidal. *Colors:* Pink, golden, yellow, green.

PROPERTIES: Brings positive view, teaches how to do only what is necessary, filters distractions, overstimulation. Enhances courage, relieves stress, calms mind. Aids organs of elimination, strengthens pulmonary and circulatory systems, increases resistance to toxins. Treats liver, heart, stomach, spine; heals concussion. Elixir treats throat infections. **Morganite (Pink Beryl):** Attracts love, maintains it. Energizes loving thoughts, actions. Activates, cleanses Heart chakra. Calms stressed life, benefits nervous system. Oxygenates cells, reorganizing them; treats T.B., asthma, emphysema, clears lungs. **Golden Beryl:** Aids scrying and magical workings.

POSITION: Place or use as appropriate.

FLU
CRY

CHRYSOBERYL

SOURCE: Australia, Brazil, Burma, Canada, Ghana, Norway.

APPEARANCE: Tabular crystals. *Colors:* Greenish-yellow, honey, red.

ADDITIONAL PROPERTIES: New beginnings, brings compassion, forgiveness. Increases spirituality, personal power, generosity, creativity, confidence. Enables seeing both sides. Highlights cause of disease. Balances adrenaline, cholesterol.

POSITION: Place as appropriate.

ALEXANDRITE

SOURCE: Russia, Sri Lanka, Brazil, Burma, Madagascar, Zimbabwe.

APPEARANCE: Variety of Chrysoberyl. *Colors:* Dark green in natural light but shines red in artificial light.

PROPERTIES: Regenerative, rebuilds self-respect, rebirth of self, inner and outer. Centers, reinforces, realigns self and mental, emotional, spiritual bodies; brings joy, expands creativity, expedites change, enhances manifestation. Emotional soother; teaches how to expend less effort. Aids nervous system, spleen, pancreas, male reproductive organs. Regenerates neurological tissue. Treats nonassimilation of protein, side effects of leukemia, relieves tension from neck muscles.

POSITION: Place as appropriate.

CHALCEDONY

SOURCE: United States, Austria, Czech Republic, Slovakia, Iceland, Mexico, New Zealand.

APPEARANCE: Transparent or opaque, sometimes banded. *Colors:* White, pinkish-brown, blue, grayish.

PROPERTIES: Promotes brotherhood, group stability, benevolence, generosity; alleviates hostility. Increases physical energy. Balances body, emotions, mind, and spirit. Eases self-doubts, facilitates constructive inward reflection. Creates open persona. Absorbs, dissipates negative energies. Cleanses, including open sores. Fosters maternal instinct, increases lactation. Improves mineral assimilation, combats mineral buildup in veins. Aids dementia and senility. **Blue Chalcedony:** Aids communication, contact, accepting new situations. Gives mental flexibility and ability to learn new languages; improves memory; aids regeneration of mucous membrane; ameliorates disease caused by weather sensitivity. Stimulates flow of lymph, lowers temperature.

POSITION: Fingers, around neck, belt buckle, place as appropriate.

CHRYSOBERYL

ALEXANDRITE

WHITE CHALCEDONY GEODE

111

OPAQUE CRYSTALS

SNOW QUARTZ

BLOODSTONE

ARAGONITE

ARAGONITE
(HEDGEHOG FORM)

SNOW QUARTZ

SOURCE: Worldwide.

APPEARANCE: Firmly compacted, milky, often water-worn. *Color:* White.

PROPERTIES: Supports learning lessons; aids letting go of responsibilities, limitations. Enhances tact, cooperation. Links to deep inner wisdom previously denied in oneself and society.

POSITION: Use anywhere.

TURQUOISE

SOURCE: United States, Egypt, Mexico, China, Iran, Peru, Poland, Russia, France, Tibet.

APPEARANCE: Opaque, often veined. *Colors:* Turquoise or blue.

PROPERTIES: Heals, protects, elevates effect, promotes spiritual attunement. Purifies, dispels negative energy. Unites earth and sky, male–female; provides healing for spirit. Empathetic, balances. Promoter of self-realization, creative problem solving. Strengthens meridians of body, subtle energy fields. Enhances physical, psychic immune systems. Alleviates pollution. Heals whole body, especially eyes.

POSITION: Anywhere.

BLOODSTONE (Heliotrope)

SOURCE: Australia, Brazil, China, Russia, India.

APPEARANCE: Green Quartz flecked with Red Jasper.

PROPERTIES: Energy cleanser, immune stimulator for acute infections. Purifies blood; detoxifies liver, kidneys, spleen. Benefits blood-rich organs, regulates bloodflow. Cleanses lower chakras, realigns energies. Gives courage. Aids recognition that chaos precedes transformation.

POSITION: Place as appropriate.

CALCITE

SOURCE: United States, Britain, Belgium, Czech Republic, Slovakia, Peru, Iceland, Romania

PROPERTIES: Translucent and waxy. *Colors:* Green, blue, yellow, orange, brown, gray, red.

PROPERTIES: Energy amplifier. Facilitates psychic abilities, channeling, astral projection, higher consciousness. Connects intellect–emotions. Alleviates emotional stress, brings serenity. Memory aid, stimulates insight. Cleanses organs, bones; strengthens skeleton, joints. **Red Calcite:** Increases energy, uplifts emotions, aids willpower. Opens Heart chakra. **Gold or Yellow Calcite:** Enhances meditation. **Orange Calcite:** Dissolves problems, maximizes potential. **Green Calcite:** Rids body of infections. Aids transition from stagnant to positive situation. Mental healer, brings balance. Aids communication. Absorbs negativity. **Rhomboid Calcite:** closes off mind chatter; heals past.

POSITION: Hold or place on appropriate point.

TURQUOISE
(NATURAL STATE)

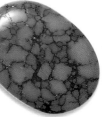

TURQUOISE
(POLISHED)

GREEN CALCITE

ARAGONITE

SOURCE: Namibia, Britain, Spain.

APPEARANCE: Chalky, fibrous, translucent, or transparent, "hedgehog" form has distinct protrusions. *Colors:* White, yellow, gold, green, blue, brown.

PROPERTIES: Earth-healer. Centers and grounds. Calming. Prepares for meditation. Raises vibration. Aids concentration, discipline and patience. Combats oversensitivity. Facilitates delegating. Warms extremities (treats Reynauds Disease). Treats chills. Heals bones, aids calcium absorption, restores elasticity to disks. Stops twitching. Strengthens immune system.

POSITION: Hold or place over affected part, or bathe with elixir. Place under pillow.

SMITHSONITE

SOURCE: Worldwide.

APPEARANCE: Lustrous, like layers of silky bubbles. *Colors:* pink, lavender, green, blue-green, purple, brown, yellow, white gray, blue.

PROPERTIES: Tranquility, charm, kindness, favorable outcomes. Heals inner child. Excellent for birth and birthing. Treats infertility. Supports leadership. Aligns chakras, strengthens psychic abilities. Heals dysfunctional immune system, sinus, and digestive disorders, osteoporosis, alcoholism. **Yellow Smithsonite:** Balances Solar Plexus chakra and mental body. Releases old hurts. Aids assimilation and skin problems. **Blue-Green Smithsonite:** Heals

emotional and other wounds with universal love, balances energy field and eases panic attacks. Aids attaining heart's desire. **Lavender Smithsonite:** Clears negative energy, aids spiritual service and higher states of consciousness, gives guidance and protection. **Pink Smithsonite:** Heals heart, abandonment and abuse, rebuilding trust and security. Aids feeling loved and supported by the universe.

POSITION: Position as appropriate. Place at crown to align chakras, Pink Smithsonite over the heart or thymus.

APATITE

SOURCE: Mexico.

APPEARANCE: Usually opaque but sometimes transparent hexagonal crystal. *Colors:* Yellow, green, gray, blue, white, purple, brown, red-brown.

PROPERTIES: Inspirational, interface of consciousness and matter; promotes humanitarian attitude, service. Stimulates creativity and intellect; eases sorrow, apathy, and anger; reduces irritability. Increases motivation and energy reserves. Induces openness and social ease—dissolves negativity and alienation. Balances physical, emotional, mental, spiritual bodies. Aids psychic development, accesses past lives, deepens meditation, raises kundalini. Heals bones, encourages formation of cells, cartilage, bone, and teeth. Ameliorates arthritis and joint problems, rickets. Suppresses hunger. **Blue Apatite:** Facilitates public speaking, enhances group communication, opens Throat chakra, heals heart. **Yellow Apatite:** Eliminator, especially toxins. Activates solar plexus. Treats M.E., lethargy, depression. Overcomes lack of concentration, inefficient learning, poor digestion. Appetite suppressant. Treats cellulite, liver, pancreas, gallbladder, spleen.

POSITION: Wear on skin over affected part.

RED CALCITE

PINK SMITHSONITE

GREEN SMITHSONITE

BLUE-GREEN APATITE

GREEN APOPHYLLITE

GREEN JADEITE

LAVENDER JADE

SOURCE: Britain, Australia, India, Brazil, Czech Republic, Slovakia, Italy.

APPEARANCE: Cubic or pyramidal. *Colors:* White, green.

PROPERTIES: Creates conscious connection between physical and spiritual realms, facilitates conscious astral travel. Promotes introspection, correction of imbalances. Aids seeing future, stimulates intuitive vision. **Green Apophyllite:** Activates Heart chakra, promotes forthright heart. Absorbs universal energy. Aids fire walks.

POSITION: Hold. For channeling, place on third eye.

JADE (Jadeite, Nephrite)

SOURCE: United States, China, Italy, Burma, Russia.

APPEARANCE: Translucent (Jadeite) or creamy (Nephrite), soapy feel.

Colors: Green, orange, brown, blue, cream, lavender, red, white.

PROPERTIES: Symbol of purity and serenity, increases love. Releases negative thoughts, soothes mind. Protects, brings harmony. "Dream stone," aids emotional release. Treats kidneys, removes toxins, rebinds cellular and skeletal systems, heals stitches. **Brown Jade:** Earths, brings comfort, reliability. Aids in adjusting to new environment. **White Jade:** Directs energy constructively, filters distractions, aids decision making. **Red Jade:** Passionate, associated with love. Accesses anger, releases tension. **Yellow Jade** Energetic, quietly stimulates, brings joy.

WHITE AND CLEAR APOPHYLLITE

Teaches interconnectedness of all beings. **Orange Jade:** Energetic, quietly stimulates, brings joy. Teaches interconnectedness. **Blue/Blue-Green Jade:** Symbolizes peace and reflection. Brings inner serenity. Aids people who feel overwhelmed by situations beyond control. **Green Jade:** Calms nervous system, channels passion in constructive ways. Harmonizes dysfunctional relationships. **Lavender Jade:** Aids emotional hurt, teaches subtlety and restraint in emotional matters.

POSITION: Place or wear as appropriate.

RHYOLITE

SOURCE: Australia, Mexico.

APPEARANCE: Banded or spotted with crystal inclusions. *Colors:* White, green, light gray, red.

PROPERTIES: Ignites potential and creativity of the soul, facilitates change, fulfills quests, aids knowing. Strengthens soul, body, and mind. Processes the past, brings in present. Enhances self-esteem. Treats veins, rashes, skin disorders, infections. Improves assimilation of B vitamins.

POSITION: Wear or position as appropriate.

NEPHRITE

JASPER

SOURCE: Worldwide.

APPEARANCE: Opaque, patterned, veined. *Colors*: Red, brown, yellow, green, blue, purple.

PROPERTIES: "Supreme nurturer." Brings tranquility, wholeness, protection; grounds. Aids quick thinking, organizational abilities, seeing projects through. Aligns chakras, facilitates shamanic journeys, dream recall. Prolongs sexual pleasure. **Brown Jasper:** Encourages environmental awareness, facilitates deep meditation, regression, centering. Gives night vision, aids astral travel.

POSITION: Forehead.

Red Jasper: Grounds energy, rectifies unjust situations. Aids dream recall. Health: strengthens circulatory system. Base chakra: aids rebirthing.

POSITION: Base chakra.

Yellow Jasper: Protects during spiritual work and physical travel. Channels positive energy, energizes endocrine system.

POSITION: Forehead, chest, throat, wrist.

Green Jasper: Heals, releases disease, obsession, skin disorders; dispels bloating. **Blue Jasper:** Connects to spiritual world. Balances yin–yang energy, stablizes aura. Sustains energy during fast, heals degenerative diseases. Balances mineral deficiency.

POSITION : Navel and Heart chakras for astral travel.

Purple Jasper: Stimulates Crown chakra. Eliminates contradictions.

POSITION: Crown as chakra.

MUSCOVITE

MUSCOVITE

SOURCE: Switzerland, Russia, Austria, Czech Republic.

APPEARANCE: Pearl-like mica. *Colors*: Pink, gray, brown, green, violet, yellow, red.

PROPERTIES: Strong angelic contact; stimulates Heart chakra, facilitates astral travel. Disperses insecurity, self-doubt, aids intuition and problem-solving. Controls blood sugar, regulates kidneys.

POSITION: Carry or hold.

APACHE TEAR
(Translucent Obsidian)

APPEARANCE: Black. Translucent when held to light, water-worn pebble.

PROPERTIES: Absorbs negative energies, protects aura. Comforts grief, provides insight into distress. Relieves grievances. Stimulates analytical capabilities and forgiveness. Removes self-limitations.

POSITION: Wear around lower chakras (men) or Heart chakra (women).

RED JASPER (RAW)

YELLOW JASPER (TUMBLED)

BLUE JASPER (TUMBLED)

RHYOLITE (NATURAL STATE)

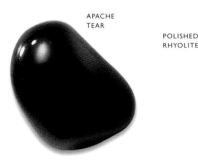

APACHE TEAR

POLISHED RHYOLITE

BLACK OBSIDIAN

**SNOWFLAKE OBSIDIAN
(TUMBLED)**

OBSIDIAN

SOURCE: Mexico.

APPEARANCE: Shiny, opaque, glasslike. *Colors:* Brown, black, blue, green, rainbow, red-black.

PROPERTIES: Grounds, protects, strengthens in times of need; helps vitalize purpose. Eliminates energy blockages, relieves tension. Stimulates growth on all levels. **Blue Obsidian:** Aids astral travel, divination, enhances telepathy. Activates throat chakra, supports communication skills. Treats speech defects, eye disorders, Alzheimer's, schizophrenia, multiple personality disorder. Alleviates pain. Heart and Throat chakras: facilitates speaking. **Electric Blue Obsidian:** Intuitive, aids divination, trance states, shamanic journeying, psychic communication, past life regression. Opens third eye, assists inner journeys. Accesses roots of difficulties, balances energy fields. Enhances radionic treatment or as a pendulum for dowsing. Makes patient more receptive. **Black Obsidian:** Grounds. Forces facing up to true self. Repels negativity, disperses unloving thoughts. Brings imbalances and shadow to surface for release. Highlights hidden factors. Increases self-control. Facilitates release of old loves. Strengthens prophesy. Provides balance during change. Used in shamanic ceremonies to remove physical disorder. **Red-Black Obsidian:** Raises kundalini energy. Promotes vitality, virility, brotherhood. Treats fevers, chills. **Rainbow Obsidian:** Cuts cords of old love, gently releases hooks others have left in heart. **Mahogany Obsidian:** Grounds and protects; gives strength in times of need; helps vitalize purpose, eliminates energy blockages, stimulates growth all levels.

POSITION: Place as appropriate.

**MAHOGANY
OBSIDIAN**

SNOWFLAKE OBSIDIAN

SOURCE: North and South America.

APPEARANCE: Mottled black and white.

PROPERTIES: Purit;, balances body, mind, spirit. Aids recognition and release of wrong thinking, ingrained patterns. Dispassion, inner centering. Treats veins, skeleton.

POSITION: Place as appropriate.

TOURMALINE

SOURCE: Sri Lanka.

APPEARANCE: Shiny, opaque or transparent, long striated or hexagonal structure. *Colors:* black, brown, green, pink, yellow, blue, watermelon, blue-green, pink, red (Rubelite).

PROPERTIES: Cleanses, purifies, transforms dense energy to lighter vibration. Grounds spiritual energy, clears chakras, forms protective shield. Releases tension, helpful in spinal adjustments. Balances male–female energy, right–left brain. Attracts inspiration, compassion, tolerance, prosperity. Tourmaline wands clear aura, remove blockages, disperse negative energy and specific problems. **Black Tourmaline:** Protects against mobile phones, electromagnetic disturbance, psychic attack, "spells," and ill-wishing. Grounds spiritual energy, increases physical vitality. Defends against debilitating disease, strengthens immune system. Treats dyslexia, arthritis.

POSITION: Around neck or between yourself and source of electromagnetics.

Black Tourmaline with Mica: Returns ill-wishing to source so perpetrator learns from it; nullifies electromagnetic smog. **Brown Tourmaline (Dravide):** Clears aura, aligns etheric body, protects it. Treats intestinal disorders.

Pink Tourmaline: Aphrodisiac. Brings love in material realm, sharing of physical pleasure. Provides assurance safe to love, inspires trust in love, confirms acceptable to love oneself. Disperses emotional pain, old destructive

BLACK TOURMALINE

WATERMELON
TOURMALINE

YELLOW TOURMALINE

GREEN TOURMALINE

feelings through Heart chakra, synthesizes love and spirituality. Promotes peace. Balances dysfunctional endocrine system.

POSITION: Place on the heart.

Red Tourmaline (Rubellite): Strengthens ability to understand love; promotes tactfulness; gives vitality to physical body; heals heart; treats digestive system, blood vessels, reproductive system. Yellow Tourmaline: Stimulates solar plexus, enhances personal power. Opens up spiritual pathway. Blue Tourmaline: Activates Throat chakra, third eye. Aids psychic awareness, promotes visions. Opens way for service to others. Benefits pulmonary and immune systems, brain. Green Tourmaline: Opens Heart chakra, promotes compassion, balance. Transforms negative to positive energy. Overcomes problems with father figures. Facilitates study of herbalism, heals plants. Treats eyes, heart, thymus, brain, immune system; facilitates weight loss; purifies; strengthens nervous system. Relieves chronic fatigue, exhaustion. Rejuvenates, inspires creativity. Purple Tourmaline: Stimulates healing heart, produces loving consciousness. Connects base and heart chakras, increasing devotion, loving aspiration. Stimulates creativity. Watermelon Tourmaline (pink enfolded in green): Aids understanding of situations. "Super-activator" of Heart chakra, links it to higher self. Treats

emotional dysfunction. Blue Tourmaline: Activates Throat chakra, third eye. Aids psychic awareness, promotes visions, opening way for service to others. Benefits pulmonary and immune systems and brain. Clear Tourmaline: Aligns meridians of physical and etheric bodies, opens Crown chakra. Synthesizes all colors.

POSITION: Place as appropriate.

AGATE

SOURCE: United States, India, Morocco, Czech Republic, Brazil, Africa.

APPEARANCE: Waxy, banded, sometimes with crystals. *Color:* Most (often artificially colored).

PROPERTIES: Grounds, improves perception and analysis. Balances yin–yang, harmonizes physical, emotional, mental, etheric. Soothes, calms. Raises consciousness, builds self-confidence. Stabilizes aura, eliminates negativity. Overcomes bitterness of heart, inner anger. Fosters love, truthfulness, courage. Pink Agate: Fosters love between parent and child.

POSITION: Hold or place on appropriate point.

BLUE LACE AGATE

SOURCE: United States, Czech Republic, Slovakia, India, Iceland, Morocco, Brazil.

APPEARANCE: Banded, lacelike. *Color:* Blue.

PROPERTIES: Calms, cools, lifts thoughts, takes spiritual inspiration to high vibration. Works on Throat, Heart, Third eye, and Crown chakras to bring about attunement. Treats arthritis, bone deformity; strengthens skeletal system; heals fractures. Aids blockages of nervous system, capillaries, pancreas. Elixir aids brain fluid imbalances, hydrocephalus.

POSITION: Place as appropriate.

AGATE
(ARTIFICIALLY COLORED)

DRAVIDE BROWN
TOURMALINE

BLUE LACE AGATE
(POLISHED)

MOSS AGATE
(TUMBLED)

FIRE AGATE

CHRYSOCOLLA

DENDRITIC AGATE

MOSS AGATE

SOURCE: United States, Australia, India.

APPEARANCE: Branching markings, like moss.
Colors: Green, blue, brown.

PROPERTIES: Cleanses circulatory and elimination systems of body. Eliminates depression caused by left–right brain imbalances. Helps intellectual people access intuitive feelings, loosen restrictions. Intuitive, creative people helps channel energy practically. Aids hypoglycemia. Elixir treats fungal infections.

POSITION: Place as appropriate.

FIRE AGATE

SOURCE: United States, Czech Republic, Slovakia, India, Iceland, Morocco, Brazil.

APPEARANCE: Slightly iridescent, glowing.
Colors: Brown and red.

PROPERTIES: Deep connection to Earth. Calms, settles energy especially before meditation. Aids introspection, brings inner problems/blocks up for examination slowly and safely, dispels fear. Reflects harm back to source to understand effect. Strong sexual connection. Alleviates stomach and endocrine problems, treats circulatory disorders, central nervous system, eyes, enhances night vision.

POSITION: Anywhere, especially on forehead.

DENDRITIC AGATE

SOURCE: United States, Czech Republic, Slovakia, India, Iceland, Morocco, Brazil.

APPEARANCE: Clear, fern-like markings. *Color*: Clear with brown markings.

PROPERTIES: Abundance. Heals Earth. Aids remaining centered in discordant situations. Treats skeletal disorders and nervous system, reverses capillary degeneration. Pain relief.

POSITION: Place as appropriate.

CHRYSOCOLLA

SOURCE: United States, Britain, Mexico, Chile, Peru, Zaire.

APPEARANCE: Opaque, often bands or inclusions. *Colors*: Green, blue, turquoise.

PROPERTIES: Tranquil; sustains, aids meditation, communication. Assists speaking truth, personal confidence, sensitivity. Calms, reenergizes chakras. At Heart chakra, heals heartache, increases capacity to love. At Throat, improves communication. Aids keeping silent when appropriate. Treats arthritis, bone disease, muscle spasm, digestive tract, ulcers, blood disorders, lung problems. Regenerates pancreas, regulates insulin and blood-sugar balance.

POSITION: Place as appropriate.

LABRADORITE

SOURCE: Italy, Greenland, Finland, Russia.

APPEARANCE: Dull until catches light, iridescent blue flashes. Yellow form transparent. *Colors*: Grayish with blue, yellow.

PROPERTIES: Protective, deflects unwanted energies from aura, prevents energy leakage. Aligns physical and etheric bodies, raises consciousness, grounds spiritual energies into body. Synthesizes intellectual thought with intuitive wisdom. Accesses spiritual purpose. Treats disorders of eyes and brain, relieves stress, regulates metabolism. **Yellow Labradorite:** Accesses highest levels of consciousness, aids trance and channeling.

POSITION: Over Higher Heart chakra.

LABRADORITE

LEPIDOLITE

MOONSTONE

TIGER'S EYE

SOURCE: Mexico, India, Australia, South Africa.

APPEARANCE: Banded, slightly shiny. *Colors*: Brown-yellow, pink, blue.

PROPERTIES: Protective, shows correct use of power. Aids accomplishing goals, recognizing inner resources, clarity of intention. Anchors change into physical body. Integrates brain hemispheres, balances yin–yang energy, energizes body. Enhances psychic abilities.

POSITION: Right arm.

HAWK'S EYE

SOURCE: United States, South Africa, India, Mexico, Australia.

APPEARANCE: Banded hawk-like "eye" (form of Tiger's Eye). *Colors*: Brown, blue.

PROPERTIES: Earths energy. Stimulates, energizes. Attracts abundance. Aids circulatory system, bowels, legs.

POSITION: Hold/place on appropriate point.

CAT'S EYE

SOURCE: United States, South Africa, India, Mexico, Australia (rare)

APPEARANCE: Banded or "eye"-like. *Color*: Yellow.

PROPERTIES: Brings confidence, happiness, serenity, good luck. Grounds, stimulates intuition, dispels negative energy from aura, protects it. Magical properties. Treats eye disorders, aids night vision. Relieves nervous headache and facial pain.

POSITION: Right arm or place as appropriate.

LEPIDOLITE

SOURCE: United States, Czech Republic, Slovakia, Brazil, Madagascar.

APPEARANCE: Platelike crystals, slightly shiny. *Color*: Purple.

PROPERTIES: Activates Throat, Heart, Third-Eye and Crown chakras, brings cosmic awareness. Stimulates intellect, reduces stress, relieves despondency and overcomes insomnia. "Stone of transition," releases and reorganizes old patterns, induces change. Restructures DNA. Enhances generation of negative ions. Excellent for menopause. Absorbs computer emanations.

POSITION: Place as appropriate.

MOONSTONE

SOURCE: India, Australia.

APPEARANCE: Milky, translucent. *Color*: White.

PROPERTIES: "New beginnings," connected to the moon. Soothes emotionality, overreactions. Reflective, makes unconscious conscious. Aids intuition, empathy, psychic abilities. Powerfully affects female reproductive cycle, balances fluids, attunes to biorhythmic clock. Aids digestive system, assimilates nutrients, eliminates toxins; alleviates degenerative conditions of skin, hair, eyes, fleshy organs, PMS symptoms. Aids conception, pregnancy, childbirth.

POSITION: Finger or appropriate body part.

HAWK'S EYE

CAT'S EYE

TIGER'S EYE
(POLISHED)

MOONSTONE

CARNELIAN
(WATER POLISHED)

SERPENTINE

CHIASTOLITE
(CROSS-SECTION)

CARNELIAN

SOURCE: Britain, India, Czech Republic, Slovakia, Peru, Iceland, Romania.

APPEARANCE: Translucent pebble, often water polished. *Colors:* Orange, red, pink.

PROPERTIES: Grounds and anchors into present surroundings. Removes fear of death, brings acceptance of cycle of life. Improves analytic abilities, clarifies perception, motivates success in business, aids positive life choices, dispels apathy. Clears extraneous thoughts in meditation, heals etheric body, protects against rage and resentment. Capacity to cleanse other crystals. Influences female reproductive organs, increases fertility. Heals lower back problems, rheumatism, arthritis, depression. Good for dramatic pursuits. Actives lower chakras. **Red Carnelian:** Stimulates weak voice. **Pink Carnelian:** Improves parent–child relationship. **Orange Carnelian:** Warms, energizes.

POSITION: Pendant. Belt buckle. Position as appropriate.

CHIASTOLITE (Cross Stone)

SOURCE: Russia.

APPEARANCE: Distinctive dark cross in center. *Colors:* Dark brown-gray-black.

PROPERTIES: Dispels negative thoughts and feelings. Transmutes conflict into harmony; aids change, problem solving. Brings creativity, answers to mysteries. Signifies death and rebirth. Facilitates astral travel. Lessens fevers, repairs chromosome damage.

POSITION: Place where appropriate or wear around neck.

CUPRITE

SERPENTINE

SOURCE: Cornwall, England, Norway, Russia, Zimbabwe.

APPEARANCE: Mottled, dual color, can be water-worn. *Colors:* Red, green.

PROPERTIES: Opens new pathways for kundalini energy. Enhances meditation; aids retrieval of wisdom, memory of past lives. Favors longevity. Eliminates parasites, aids calcium and magnesium absorption.

POSITION: Hold or place on appropriate spot.

CUPRITE

SOURCE: United States, Britain, Germany, France, Namibia, Peru.

APPEARANCE: Small crystal mass. *Color:* Red. Philosophical, teaches helpfulness to others. Overcomes difficulties in dealing with father or authoritarian figures, strengthens will. Facilitates past-life investigation. Stimulates Base chakra, grounds energy, revitalizes physical energy. Aids heart and blood, muscle tissue, and skeletal system; oxygenates; overcomes metabolic imbalances. Treats AIDS, blood disorders, water retention, bladder and kidney malfunction, vertigo, altitude sickness. Helps overcome fear of terminal conditions.

POSITION: As appropriate.

AVENTURINE

SOURCE: Italy, Brazil, China, India, Russia, Tibet, Nepal.

APPEARANCE: Opaque, speckled with shiny particles. *Colors*: Green, blue, red.

PROPERTIES: Enhances creativity, brings prosperity. Absorbs electromagnetic stress. Diffuses negativity, balances male–female energy. Aids seeing alternatives, possibilities. Promotes growth from birth to seven years. Benefits thymus gland and nervous system. Balances blood pressure. Elixir aids skin problems. **Blue Aventurine**: Mental healer. **Green Aventurine**: Works on Heart chakra; activates, cleans, protects. Shields from loss of heart energy. Useful healer for body, attracts mature love.

POSITION: Hold or place on appropriate point.

RHODONITE

SOURCE: Spain, Russia, Sweden, Germany.

APPEARANCE: Mottled, often flecked with black. *Color*: Pink.

PROPERTIES: Grounds, balances yin–yang; shows both sides of issue. Stimulates, clears, activates Heart Chakra. Balances physical and mental energies. Nurtures love. Encourages brotherhood of humanity. Useful for trauma. Aids confidence, alleviates confusion. Benefits communication, opens third eye. Aligns physical and etheric bodies, maintains good health. Balances male–female energy. Beneficial in osteoporosis, tooth decay, calcium deficiency, calcium deposits. Dissipates blocks in nervous system, relieves muscle spasm.

POSITION: Place as appropriate.

GREEN AVENTURINE
(POLISHED)

RHODOCHROSITE

RHODOCHROSITE

SOURCE: United States, Russia.

APPEARANCE: Banded. *Colors*: Pink to orange.

PROPERTIES: Selfless love and compassion, improves self-worth, integrates spiritual and material energies. Expands consciousness, clears Solar Plexus chakra, enhances dream states. Alleviates irrational fear, paranoia. Teaches heart to assimilate painful feelings without shutting down, removes denial. Attracts soulmate. Irritant filter: aids asthma, respiratory problems. Purifies circulatory system, kidneys, restores poor eyesight. Elixir relieves infections, balances thyroid.

POSITION: Wrist or heart.

SUGILITE (Luvulite)

SOURCE: Japan, South Africa.

APPEARANCE: Opaque, lightly banded, or translucent. *Color*: Purple.

PROPERTIES: Represents spiritual love, opens chakras to flow of love. Brings spiritual awareness, positive thoughts, promotes channeling ability. Protects soul from shocks and disappointments. Aids forgiveness, eliminates hostility. Excellent for autism, learning difficulties. Aids misfits. Promotes understanding of effect of mind on body. Resolves group difficulties. Benefits cancer sufferers. Place on third eye to alleviate despair. Clears headaches and discomfort.

POSITION: Place as appropriate, especially over the heart.

SUGILITE
(TUMBLED)

BLUE AVENTURINE
(NATURAL STATE)

RHODONITE
(POLISHED)

CHRYSOPRASE

VARISCITE (POLISHED)

CHRYSOPRASE

SOURCE: United States, Russia, Brazil, Australia, Poland, Tanzania.

APPEARANCE: Opaque, flecked. *Color:* Apple green.

PROPERTIES: Relaxation, peaceful sleep. Promotes hope, gives personal insight. Calming, non-egotistical, creates openness to new situations. Draws out talents, stimulates creativity. Energizes Heart chakra and body. Enhances fertility, said to guard against sexually transmitted diseases. Aids gout, eye problems, mental illness; treats heart problems, ameliorates general infirmity.

POSITION: Place as appropriate.

MALACHITE

SOURCE: Romania, Zambia, Zaire, Russia.

APPEARANCE: Concentric light and dark bands. *Color:* Green.

PROPERTIES: Brings transformation; draws out deep feelings; breaks unwanted ties, outworn patterns. Clears, activates chakras; clarifies emotions; releases negative experiences. Combined with Azurite aids visualization and psychic vision. Gives responsibility for one's actions, thoughts, and feelings. Absorbs plutonium pollution, guards against radiation. Treats asthma, arthritis, fractures, swollen joints, growths, tumors. Aligns DNA and cellular structure, enhances immune system. (Use polished Malachite for elixir preparation.)

POSITION: Place on the left hand or position on third eye.

VARISCITE

SOURCE: United States, Germany, Austria, Czech Republic, Slovakia, Bolivia.

APPEARANCE: Opaque, veined. *Color:* Greenish with brown veins.

PROPERTIES: Gives encouragement, hope and courage useful with illness and invalids. Aids past life exploration. Heals nervous system; treats abdominal distention, constricted blood flow; regenerates elasticity of veins. Helpful for male impotence.

POSITION: Place as appropriate.

UNAKITE

SOURCE: South Africa.

APPEARANCE: Mottled. *Color:* Green-pink.

PROPERTIES: Vision. Balances emotions with spirituality. Facilitates rebirthing, integrates information from past that creates blockages, gently releases conditions that inhibit growth. Reaches root cause of disease. Treats reproductive system, creates weight gain, aids healthy pregnancy.

POSITION: Place as appropriate.

UNAKITE (UNPOLISHED)

MALACHITE (POLISHED)

AZURITE (ON MATRIX WITH MALACHITE)

LAPIS LAZULI

SOURCE: Russia, Afghanistan, Chile, Italy, United States, Egypt.

APPEARANCE: Opaque, flecked with gold. *Color:* Deep blue.

PROPERTIES: Protects, enlightens, enhances dream work, psychic abilities. Quickly releases stress, brings deep peace. Powerful thought amplifier. Stimulates higher faculties of mind, promotes objectivity, clarity. Promotes creativity, attunement to source. Contacts spirit guardians. Harmonizes physical, emotional, mental, and spiritual levels. Alleviates pain, migraine. Helps overcome depression. Benefits respiratory system, throat; cleanses organs, bone marrow, thymus, and immune system. Overcomes hearing loss. Purifies blood, boosts immune system. Alleviates insomnia, vertigo.

POSITION: Throat or third eye.

AZURITE

SOURCE: United States, Australia, Chile, Peru, France, Namibia, Russia.

APPEARANCE: Very small, shiny crystals (not visible when tumbled). *Color:* Blue, sometimes with green (Malachite).

PROPERTIES: Stimulates third eye; facilitates psychic development, spiritual guidance, higher consciousness, clear understanding. Releases long-standing blocks in communication, stimulates memory. Brings new perspectives, expands mind. Treats arthritis, joint problems; aligns spine.

POSITION: Right hand or place as appropriate.

SODALITE

SODALITE

SOURCE: North America, France, Brazil, Greenland, Russia, Burma, Romania.

APPEARANCE: Mottled dark and light blue-white. *Color:* Blue.

PROPERTIES: Unites logic and intuition, eliminates mental confusion. Encourages rational thought, objectivity, truth, intuitive perception, verbalization of feelings. Calms mind, allows new information to be received. Brings about emotional balance. Aids group work. Balances metabolism. Benefits and cleanses organs, boosts immune system. Combats radiation and insomnia.

POSITION: As appropriate.

ANTACAMITE

SOURCE: Unites States.

APPEARANCE: Tiny crystals on matrix—resembles Chrysocolla. *Color:* Turquoise.

PROPERTIES: Opens third eye. Creates powerful images and strong spiritual connection. Restores spiritual trust and connection to higher guidance. Aids kidneys and elimination.

POSITION: Place on third eye.

CHAROITE

SOURCE: Russia.

APPEARANCE: Mottled and veined. *Color:* Purple.

PROPERTIES: Transformation. Synthesizes Heart and Crown chakras, cleanses aura, stimulates unconditional love. Aids decision making. Integrates "negative qualities," facilitates acceptance of others. Transmutes energy, converts disease to health. Grounds spiritual self. Heals, integrates dualities. Treats eyes, heart, liver, pancreas. Regulates blood pressure. Alleviates aches and pains.

POSITION: Over heart.

LAPIS LAZULI

ANTACAMITE
(ON MATRIX)

CHAROITE

JET
(POLISHED)

LARIMAR

SARDONYX

ONYX
(POLISHED)

JET

SOURCE: Worldwide, especially United States.

APPEARANCE: Coal-like, usually polished. *Color:*
Black.

PROPERTIES: Draws out negative energy,
unreasonable fears. Promotes control of life,
fights mood swings, depression. Protects against
violence, illness. Stabilizes finances. Increases
virility. Treats migraine, epilepsy, swellings, colds.

POSITION: Anywhere, set in silver.

LARIMAR

(Dolphin Stone/Pectolite)

SOURCE: Dominican Republic, Bahamas.

APPEARANCE: Smooth, with whorls of color or
white veins (form of Pectolite). *Colors:* Blue,
blue-green, gray, or red with white.

PROPERTIES: Brings serenity and clarity, and
deeply meditative consciousness. Earth-healing
stone. Removes self-constraints, dissolves
sacrificial behavior, aids taking control of life.
Finds true pathway. Brings out untouched
"angelic inner child." Facilitates cleansing tears.
Radiates love and peace. Useful for guilt.
Removes entities. Stimulates Third eye, Heart,
Crown and Throat chakras, and self-healing.
Heals cartilage and throat conditions. Treats
feet—excellent reflexology tool.

POSITION: Hold or wear for prolonged periods,
use on feet.

SARDONYX

SOURCE: Brazil, India, Russia, Asia Minor.

APPEARANCE: Banded, opaque. *Colors:* black, red,
brown, clear.

PROPERTIES: Strength, protection. Increases
stamina, vigor, self-control. Lasting happiness in
marriage, attracts friends, lifts depression. Heals
lungs, bones. **Brown Sardonyx:** Grounds energy.
Clear Sardonyx: Purification. **Black Sardonyx:**
Absorbs negativity. **Red Sardonyx:** Stimulates.

POSITION: Anywhere.

ONYX

SOURCE: Italy, Mexico, United States, Russia,
Brazil.

APPEARANCE: Banded. *Colors:* Black, gray.

PROPERTIES: Strength-giving, beneficial during
difficult or confusing periods. Centers, aligns
with higher power. Promotes vigor, stamina,
steadfastness, wise decisions. Aids learning
lessons, imparts self-confidence, ease in
surroundings. Mental tonic, aids fears, worries.
Recognizes, integrates dualities. Helps teeth,
bones, bone marrow, blood disorders, feet.

POSITION: Left side of body.

PYROLUSITE

SOURCE: United States, Britain, Brazil, India.

APPEARANCE: Shiny, fanlike on brown matrix.
Color: Silver.

PROPERTIES: Restructures life, heals
disturbances. Gets to bottom of problems.
Changes, stabilizes relationships. Transmutes
physical, emotional, mental bodies. Promotes
confidence, optimism, determination. Dispels
psychic interference. Treats bronchitis, regulates
metabolism, strengthens blood vessels,
stimulates sexuality.

POSITION: Place as appropriate.

PYROLUSITE
(ON MATRIX)

HEMATITE

MAGNETITE (Lodestone)

SOURCE: United States, India, Mexico, Romania, Italy, Finland, Austria.

APPEARANCE: Dark and grainy (iron ore).
Colors: Dark brown, black

PROPERTIES: Aids telepathy, visualization and balanced perspective. Connects to nurturing aspect of Earth. Attracts love. Beneficial for blood and circulatory system. Stimulates sluggish organs and sedates overactive. Useful for sports injuries, relieves aches and pains.

POSITION: Place on back of neck and base of spine, or on aching joint.

HEMATITE
(POLISHED)

BOJI STONES
(MALE ABOVE –
FEMALE BELOW)

HEMATITE

SOURCE: Britain, Italy, Brazil, Sweden, Canada, Switzerland.

APPEARANCE: "Brainlike," red or gray (polished).
Colors: Silver or gray (unpolished), red.

PROPERTIES: Grounds, protects, and balances, boosts self-esteem and survival ability. Aids concentration, focus, will power, reliability, confidence. Enhances memory, original thought. Removes self-limitations. Yang: balances meridians. Dissolves negativity. Benefits legal situations. Supports timid women. Strongly affects blood, aids anemia, supports kidneys, cleanses blood. Treats leg cramps, nervous disorders, insomnia. Aids spinal alignment, healing of fractures.

POSITION: Base and top of spine.

CHRYSANTHEMUM STONE

SOURCE: China, Japan, Canada, United States.

POSITION: Resembles the chrysanthemum flower. *Color:* Various.

PROPERTIES: Drifts through time, exudes calm confidence; synthesizes change with harmony, enjoyment of present moment, inspires, energizes. Stimulates impetuous self-development. Overcomes bigotry, ignorance, narrow-mindedness, self-righteousness, jealousy. Brings endeavors to fruition. Treats skin, skeleton, eyes; disperses toxins.

POSITION: Wear, carry, or place in the environment. Use as an elixir.

MAGNETITE
(ON MATRIX)

BOJI STONE

SOURCE: United States, Britain.

APPEARANCE: Metallic looking, smooth (female) or with square protrusions (male). *Color:* Brown but some blue.

PROPERTIES: Grounds back into reality after spiritual activity. Protective function.

POSITION: Hold or carry.

CHRYSANTHEMUM
STONE

FURTHER READING

CRYSTALS:

GIENGER, MICHAEL, *Crystal Power, Crystal Healing,* Cassell & Co. London 1998

HALL, JUDY, *The Illustrated Guide to Crystals,* Godsfield Press/Sterling Publications 2000

LILY, SIMON, *Healing With Crystals,* Southwater 2001

MELODY, *LOVE IS IN THE EARTH,* Earth Love Publishing House, Colorado, 1995

RAPHAELL, KATRINA, *Crystal Healing Vols 1, II, III,* Aurora Press, Sante Fe 1987

RAVEN, HAZEL, *Crystal Healing: The Complete Practitioner's Guide,* Raven & Co, Manchester 2000

DIVINATION:

HALL, JUDY, *The Illustrated Guide to Divination,* Godsfield Press/Sterling Publications 2000

HALL, JUDI, *What's My Future?* Penguin Books 2000

ASTROLOGY:

HALL, JUDY, *The Illustrated Guide to the Zodiac,* Sterling Publications 1999

HALL, JUDY, *Patterns of the Past: The Birthchart, Karma and Reincarnation,* Wessex Astrologer 2000

HALL, JUDY, *Karmic Connections: The Birthchart, Karma and Relationships,* Wessex Astrologer 2001

PSYCHIC PROTECTION:

HALL, JUDY, *The Art of Psychic Protection,* Samuel Weiser 1995

HALL, JUDY, *The Way of Psychic Protection,* HarperCollins Publishers 1999

ACKNOWLEDGMENTS

The publishers are grateful to the following for permission to reproduce copyright material:

CORBIS pps *62–63, 73, 101;* CORBIS STOCKMARKET pp *54*

Bridgewater Book Company would like to thank Sapphire Crystals, Cliffe High Street, Lewes, East Sussex, U.K. for the loan of the large Chinese Quartz and other assorted crystals shown on the front cover. In addition, the assistance of the staff at Earthworks, Poole, has been invaluable in compiling this book and sourcing appropriate crystals.

The publishers would also like to thank Judy Hall for permission to reproduce material from The Zodiac Pack.

For suppliers of Crystal Clear e-mail estoe@yahoo.dot.com

INDEX

abundance 28, 58–9
addictions 10, 44
adrenal glands 32–3
affinities 97
affirmations 12, 17, 59
agate 19, 22, 26, 43, 47, 55, 66, 74, 117
ailments 36–7, 88, 90–5
alexandrite 111
amazonite 24, 57, 64, 65, 73
amber 33, 43, 47, 55, 71, 74, 109
ambience 54
amethyst 14–15, 19, 20, 21, 22, 24, 26, 33, 34, 35, 36, 38, 42, 45, 47, 54, 56, 62, 70, 71, 72, 73, 74, 75, 78, 105
ametrine 24, 33, 71, 74, 106
angelite 54, 66, 71, 109
antacamite 24, 123
Apache tear 66, 70, 71, 72, 73, 74, 115
apatite 24, 43, 47, 55, 56, 57, 113
apophyllite 21, 24, 33, 37, 45, 114
aqua aura 24, 33, 38, 40, 70, 106
aquamarine 26, 33, 38, 42, 45, 56, 57, 74, 101
Aquarius 37, 87
aragonite 33, 38, 47, 72, 74, 113
Aries 36, 82
astrology 31, 80–7
attitude 56
aura 40–1, 70–1, 88, 98
aventurine 19, 33, 37, 38, 62, 63, 67, 70, 71, 75, 121
azeztulite 24, 75, 77, 106
azurite 22, 24, 38, 47, 57, 123

balance 42, 43, 50, 67, 96
balls 10, 14, 20–1
baths 30, 37–8, 45, 50, 63
beryl 14, 20, 22, 33, 46, 63, 67, 110
birthstones 31, 80–7
bitterness 44
black agate 19
blockages 10, 40–1, 60, 65
blood pressure 34
bloodstone 19, 26, 37, 38, 48, 59, 112
blue lace agate 19, 42, 57, 67, 117
boji stone 25, 74, 125
bowls 34, 56

calcite 24, 33, 34, 37, 38, 45, 46, 47, 48, 54, 74, 112
Cancer 36, 83
Capricorn 37, 86
care of crystals 76–9
carnelian 17, 46, 56, 59, 63, 70, 74, 76, 77, 120
cars 74
cat's eye 14, 119
celestite 24, 44, 54, 71, 108
chakras 37, 40–1, 50, 60, 65, 67, 88, 96
chalcedony 33, 37, 38, 43, 44, 45, 46, 47, 56, 74, 111
charoite 33, 36, 48, 74, 123
chiastolite 64, 74, 120
childhood traumas 43, 66
choosing crystals 9, 20, 31
chrysanthemum stone 53, 125
chrysoberyl 44, 111
chrysocolla 33, 44, 66, 67, 118
chrysolite 43
chrysoprase 34, 46, 57, 67, 121
citrine 19, 34, 35, 37, 43, 47, 50, 55, 56, 58, 59, 64, 70, 74, 77, 78, 109
cleansing 31, 77–9
clear crystals 104–11
communication 56
compromise 56
computers 54, 72
concentration 12, 45, 50
confidence 32–3, 42, 44
conflict 56
cooperation 56
crime 68
criticism 56
cuprite 120

danburite 47, 67, 108
dedication 16
delegation 33
dendritic agate 37, 54, 58, 59, 118
depression 43, 74
desks 56
diamond 19, 26, 42, 47, 59, 63, 64, 100
dioptase 26, 34, 38, 46, 67, 106–7
directory 88–125
dowsing 48, 49, 72
dreams 26–7

eating disorders 44
electromagnetic pollution 72–3
elixirs 50–1, 99
emerald 14, 19, 26, 42, 56, 63, 64, 101
emotional well-being 42–3, 66, 74
energy transmission 8, 37, 65
engagement rings 63
environmental smog 30, 72–3
exhaustion 37
eyestrain 57

Feng Shui 55, 59
finding love 62–3
fire agate 71, 118
fluorite 42, 43, 45, 47, 54, 56, 63, 64, 72, 73, 74, 110
forgiveness 44
formation 8

garnet 19, 37, 59, 63, 64, 102
gem remedies 30, 38–9, 50–1, 88, 99
Gemini 36, 83
gemstones 100–3
geodes 10
geopathic stress 30, 49, 68, 72, 73
grids 34–35, 38–9, 41, 45, 48–9, 55, 65, 67, 75, 96
grounding 25, 33, 74, 96
guide 88, 100–25
guilt 44

hawk's eye 58, 59, 119
headaches 36, 40
healing 30–1
heart chakra 60, 67, 96
hematite 19, 44, 47, 74, 79, 125
Herkimer diamond 33, 49, 72, 73, 75, 109
hiddenite 109
holes in aura 40, 70
home use 52–4, 74
houseplants 52, 54

ill-wishing 68, 71
immune system 32, 33, 38–9
infections 38
insomnia 33, 49, 75
intent 12
internal use 30, 50–1
intuition 18, 21, 24–5, 57